Halos of Fire

$\mathcal{H}$alos ^{of} $\mathcal{F}$ire

Enjoying a Life filled with
the Power of the Holy Spirit

John Connell

The
Olive Press
Savannah, Georgia

Halos of Fire: Enjoying a Life Filled with the Power of the Holy Spirit
By John Connell
Published by The Olive Press

The Olive Press
P.O. Box 14196, Savannah, GA. 31411
Unless otherwise noted, all Scripture quotations are taken from the New American Standard Bible. Copyright © 1995 by The Lockman Foundation (www.lockman.org) and used with permission.
Feedback to the author: john@johnsconnell.com
For information regarding special discounts for bulk purchases, please contact Buhrmaster Marketing at (773) 481-4964 or specialsales@theolivepress.net

Cover and interior design by Pneuma Books, LLC
Visit www.pneumabooks.com

8 7 6 5 4 3 2 1   05 06 07 08 09

Publisher's Cataloging-in-Publication Data
(Prepared by The Donohue Group, Inc.)

Connell, John.
   Halos of fire : enjoying a life filled with the power of the Holy Spirit / John Connell.-- [1st ed.]
   p. cm. -- (The living with power library ; v. 1)
   Includes bibliographical references and index.
ISBN-13: 978-09717330-8-4
ISBN-10: 0-9717330-8-2

   1. Holy Spirit. 2. Inspiration--Religious aspects--Christianity.
3. Christian life. I. Title.

BT123 .C66 2004   231.3
2004101798

Table of Contents

Dedication

For my grandson, Cooper Connell Davis, and my grand-daughter, Grace Duval Davis. An injury on August 23, 2002, left our one-year-old Cooper vegetative, and our precious Gracie was ushered into heaven on February 18, 2004, after struggling four months and three days for life. God has used these priceless children to teach me utter dependence on the Holy Spirit who strengthens me in my weakness and intercedes on my behalf with groanings too deep for words. In the midst of pain, the Spirit has caused rivers of living water to flow out of my innermost being.

Foreword

I am a relatively new Christian. I accepted Jesus Christ as my Lord and Savior as a result of the trials I have endured since the loss of my husband in the terrorist attacks on the World Trade Center on 9/11. Prior to the tragedy, I was not well-grounded biblically. My religious upbringing consisted primarily of the knowledge that there undoubtedly *is* a God, but my relationship with Him on 9/11 was limited and immature. I truly believe that since then God has sanctified my life through His grace and intervention. I was baptized on October 5, 2003, and I have completely surrendered my life to Him.

Three years ago, I did not even own a Bible. Now, I cannot get enough of it. I thirst for the Word, and God has me on the fast forward track. I have immersed myself in Him, and I have learned so much in such a short time. Yet there is still so much I do not understand.

Halos of Fire has helped me to bridge many of the gaps in my knowledge of God and His ways. What may seem like fundamental concepts to a veteran Christian are often complicated issues for me since I do not have a strong scriptural foundation. I've read many books, I attend many Bible studies, and I have a good relationship with my pastor (G. Richard Fisher of Laurelton Park Baptist Church) who kindly and patiently instructs me. But *Halos of Fire* was different. It literally made the light bulb go on.

This book brought me to tears as I recognized how often my emotions and experiences are actually the work of the Spirit inside me. It also made me laugh, because the writing is so lighthearted and palpable. And there were times when I actually yelled out, "Yes!" bursting with joy and gratitude because it all finally made so much sense.

I pray that everyone who reads *Halos of Fire* will be enlightened as I have been. I pray that the Spirit will accomplish great work through you, His willing servant. And I pray that you will find peace and healing through God's loving embrace.

This book teaches us how to open ourselves to God's awaiting arms, and it reintroduces us to the awesome power of the Holy Spirit dwelling within us. *Halos of Fire* is a spiritual alarm clock, jolting us awake to a stronger biblical understanding and a closer relationship to the Holy Spirit and the promises of God. This book has opened my eyes to God's divine purpose and His extraordinary gifts to us in a way I never thought possible and for which I am deeply, deeply grateful.

In His love,
Jennifer Sands
9/11 widow, author of *A Tempered Faith*

$\mathscr{P}$reface

"This book changed my life. It took God out of my head and put Him into my heart." Those are the words of David Taylor, editor at The Olive Press, upon accepting this book for publication. I rejoiced when I heard them because I knew God was at work, using the book as His tool. But David's words also echoed the New Testament book of Acts, from which *Halos of Fire* springs.

The book of Acts has been referred to by one scholar as the New Testament's "pivotal book," and by another scholar as the New Testament's "most important book." In my view, Acts stands as the New Testament's centerpiece because it forms what might be called "the headwaters" of God's movement among His followers in the twenty-first century. In the book of Acts the church of Jesus Christ is born. Acts spells out the charter of the church and provides its identity. Not only that, but the book of Acts also supplies the gene pool from which the individual follower of Christ draws his or her sanctified DNA.

Neither a church nor an individual can truly impact a community or a world without constantly bathing in the Church's headwaters. Plunging into those waters, a person quickly discovers the express purpose of the Church and of life itself — a purpose spelled out in the five words that comprise the heart of Acts 1:8, "You shall be My witnesses." Those five words say at least three things to the Christian:

1. We are a fellowship of men and women who center everything on the living Christ.

2. We are to extend the work and ministry of Jesus Christ. What Jesus began we must continue.

3. We are to focus on persuading others to link their lives to Jesus Christ. Following Him means inviting others to follow Him as well.

DYNAMITE FOR LIVING

As we bathe in the headwaters of the church we not only discover the express purpose of the Church and life itself, we also discover the explosive power that belongs to the church and to the men and women who comprise it. This power is the guiding light of *Halos of Fire*. What is this power's source?

One of the most exciting promises made by Jesus appears in Acts 1:8: "You will receive power when the Holy Spirit has come upon you!" You have, no doubt, heard of the Nobel Peace Prize — an annual award established by Swedish chemist, Alfred Nobel. What you may not know is that in 1867 Alfred Nobel produced what was, at that time, the most powerful explosive in the world. Nobel asked a scholar of the New Testament if the Greek language had a word for explosive power. The answer came back: *dunamis.* Thus, Nobel named his explosive substance *dynamite.* The word translated *power* in Acts 1:8 is taken from the Greek word *dunamis.* Jesus promises that you will receive *dunamis,* that is, you shall receive explosive power!

Wouldn't you like to experience this explosive power that Jesus guaranteed to those who follow Him? Isn't it time to step out of an anemic, impotent version of Christianity that has been more of a hindrance than a help? You don't have to live one more day as a debilitated, puny, apologetic harbinger of spiritual inadequacy. *Halos of Fire* was written with practicality in mind, and that's critical. No matter how reliable a book may be in its content, if it is not relevant to daily living then it is not useful in our lives.

If you're interested in what might be called spiritual genetics, you're holding in your hand a book that will help you decipher the cellular codes that, up until now, have been more like gibberish than life-giving insights. In every chapter, I have tried to provide clear, eye-opening ideas that can be readily applied and perennially enjoyed. As Paul wrote in I Corinthians 14:7, "If there is not a distinction in the tones, how can anyone know precisely what tune the band is playing?" My hope is that in each chapter you will not only hear the tune clearly, but you will find yourself spontaneously dancing to the music.

THE POWER FOR *L*IVING LIBRARY

PART ONE

What They Celebrated

Then the Spirit of the LORD will come upon you mightily, and you shall ... be changed into another man.

—

1 Samuel 10:6

Chapter One

Changed *into* Another Man

*Blow back the cold, gray ashes covering the red-hot ember of the
Holy Spirit and expose yourself to the divine glow.*

In this chapter you will learn:

* The explosive power within you
* The revolutionary promise of God to you
* How Jesus empowers each of His followers
* How to give up your spiritual security blanket

To me, the greatest shock of today's church is that after 2,000
years of Christianity most followers of Jesus Christ have no
idea—not a single clue—about the explosive power promised
in Acts and residing in their lives today. They are like the disciples of John whom Paul questioned at Ephesus. Paul asked
them: "Did you receive the Holy Spirit when you believed?"

Their reply: "We have not even heard whether there is a
Holy Spirit" (Acts 19:2).

I agree with A. W. Tozer, who is quoted as saying: "If the
Holy Spirit were withdrawn from our churches today, 95

1

percent of what we do would go on and no one would know the difference."[1] Isn't 95 percent dangerously close to 100, when the Holy Spirit would be totally inactive in our churches and our lives?

Jesus came to embrace us. But that is only half of the story. Jesus also wants to empower us in every facet of our lives— whether we are sharing our faith or showing our faith. How does Jesus empower His followers? At the same time God called the church into existence, He also gave to the church a Companion who would energize every person who comprised the church. Jesus did not say, "You shall be My witnesses, now go out there and do the best you can."

Jesus told them: You will be My witnesses, and I'm going to give you an Enabler who will make you highly effective in serving Me. I'm not going to leave you to your own ability. I'm going to give you supernatural ability.

Who is this Companion, this Enabler? Acts 1:8 says, "You will receive power when the Holy Spirit has come upon you." Jesus is saying to His followers, to you and to me: Listen, there is going to come a moment when the Holy Spirit will overtake your life, and through His explosive power you will be given a remarkable ability to go forth as My witnesses.

LIKE A THOUSAND ROLLING RIVERS: SAY HELLO TO THE HOLY SPIRIT

I wonder if those who stood with Jesus that day truly knew what He meant. I wonder if they had any inkling as to what was about to take place. Jesus had tried repeatedly to prepare them for the coming of this explosive power by focusing their attention on this amazing ability that would overtake their lives. In Acts 1:4, Jesus reminded His disciples that He had instructed them in the past about the Holy Spirit. In fact, the Holy Spirit had been a major topic of conversation between Jesus and His disciples.

What had Jesus taught His disciples about the Holy Spirit?

- That the Holy Spirit would be like a Father to them.
- That the Holy Spirit would be a helper and a teacher.
- That the Holy Spirit would inhabit their innermost being.
- That His presence would flow from their hearts like a thousand rolling rivers.

Jesus tells his followers in Acts 1:5 that they would soon be baptized with the Holy Spirit, that they would be totally immersed into the sphere of the Holy Spirit, drenched and saturated with His energy. As the Holy Spirit had come upon Him, so the Holy Spirit would come upon them. As the Holy Spirit had empowered Him, so the Holy Spirit would empower them.

Clearly, Jesus proclaimed to His followers that something extraordinary was about to take place in their lives. Of course, what Jesus proclaimed to His disciples had already been promised by His Father more than eight hundred years before. In Acts 1:4, Jesus told his followers to gather in Jerusalem and wait for what the Father had promised.

What had the Father promised? Normally, we would have to go all the way back to the Old Testament prophet, Joel, to make that discovery. In his letter to Theophilus, Luke outlines God's promise, which was first revealed to the Old Testament prophet Joel: "'It shall be in the last days,' God says, 'that I will pour forth of My Spirit upon all mankind'" (Acts 2:17).

A GOD OF REVOLUTION

This promise from God is nothing short of revolutionary. Prior to that moment, the Holy Spirit had not been given indiscriminately to God's people, but selectively. Search the pages of the Old Testament and you will discover that only a few people knew, firsthand, the explosive power of the Spirit. Joseph and

Moses knew. Joshua, Samson, Samuel, and Elijah knew. Saul and David certainly knew. But only a few had experienced the might and strength of the Holy Spirit. The vast majority of God's people in the Old Testament had no idea about this amazing phenomenon. Yet, in 835 BC, God promised: There is going to come a day when I will pour out My Spirit upon all who come to Me. I will lavish My Spirit upon them like an unending downpour of rain.

A revolutionary promise, indeed. Yet, it becomes even more revolutionary:

> And your sons and your daughters shall prophesy, and your young men shall see visions, and your old men shall dream dreams; even upon My bondslaves, both men and women, I will in those days pour forth of My Spirit and they shall prophesy (Joel 2:28).

Not only would God pour forth His Spirit upon men but also upon women.

Unheard of!

Not only would God pour forth His Spirit upon the titan but also upon the tottering.

How wasteful!

Not only would God pour forth His Spirit upon the experienced but upon the inexperienced.

Ridiculous!

Not only would God pour forth His Spirit upon the politically free but upon the politically fettered.

Impossible!

Someone dared to write that the Spirit would be given *without distinction of sex . . . without distinction of age . . . without distinction of rank. . . .* and that *even the slaves would be exalted.*

Unexpected. Unparalleled. Unthinkable. Yet true. The

Holy Spirit would burst through every barrier and quicken the energies of life in all who would believe.

THE PROPHET WITHIN YOU

What can people do when the Holy Spirit comes pouring into their lives? Verses 17 and 18 of Acts 2 tell us. They can *dream dreams*, *see visions*, and *prophesy*. That means no less than two things. First, you can understand and apply scriptural truth to the circumstances of your life. Second, you can, as Peter said, "proclaim the excellencies of Him who called you out of darkness into His marvelous light" (1 Pet. 2:9). In essence, you can become a kind of prophet, not only living God's will, but revealing His message to others.

That which was promised by the Father and proclaimed by the Son came to fruition in the second chapter of Acts. On the day of Pentecost an exciting new age began for the followers of Christ. Beginning with that moment, everyone who becomes a disciple of Jesus Christ is immersed into the world of the Holy Spirit. From that point forward, everyone who becomes a disciple of Jesus Christ is given the ability not only to absorb the truth of God's Word, but the ability to inspire others to follow Him as a way of life—to be a dreamer, a visionary, a prophet.

HOW TO WEAR YOUR HALO OF FIRE

Charles Schulz, creator of the *Peanuts* comic strip, was a Christian who often incorporated subtle bits of biblical truth into his work. During an interview on National Public Radio's *Morning Edition*, Schultz was asked if the Great Pumpkin would ever show up for Linus, who waits expectantly each Halloween. Schulz replied that Linus's hope would never be fulfilled because the Great Pumpkin is fictional, something that Linus dreamed up and cannot admit is of his own making. Linus is trapped in a belief he refuses to give up, Schultz explained. Most of all, Linus is confusing Halloween with Christmas—the real season of looking for someone from above.

You may know the difference between Halloween and Christmas, but do you know the difference between dead intellectualism and Pentecost? In this book I ask you to do something bold, something Linus would not do: Give up your security blanket and open your heart and mind to the presence and power of the Holy Spirit. Blow back the cold, gray ashes covering the red-hot ember of the Spirit and expose yourself to the divine glow.

How?

First, in its text and through a series of exercises, this book teaches you how to rehearse daily the reality of the Spirit's presence in your life and how to think and talk about His presence to your family, your friends, and, most of all, to your heavenly Father.

Second, this book also encourages you to take chances:

- to risk the reality of the Spirit's power in everything you think, say, and do;
- to attempt what you never dreamed of attempting;
- to accomplish what you never dreamed of accomplishing; and
- to impact the lives of those around you in ways you never thought possible.

When Samuel anointed Saul as Israel's first king, he said to Saul, "The Spirit of the Lord will come upon you mightily, and you shall . . . be changed into another man. . . . do for yourself what the occasion requires, for God is with you" (1 Sam. 10:6-7).

That same Spirit is available for you right now. The Holy Spirit is not merely for the so-called charismatic community.

The Holy Spirit is for anyone and everyone who is a follower of Jesus Christ. My prayer is that your study of this book will result in an ongoing experience of spiritual power and exuberance that will enable you to serve the Lord with undeniable effectiveness and grace until at last you see Him face-to-face.

May you discover the Holy Spirit anew.

May you always wear your halo of fire.

NOTES

[1] A. W. Tozer, As quoted by Alan Redpath in *Christian Life* magazine, *Christianity Today*, vol. 29.

The Holy Spirit Workout # 1:

DETERMINE YOUR HSRQ:
(HOLY SPIRIT READINESS QUOTIENT)

The purpose of this book is to lead you to become a dreamer, a visionary, and a proclaimer of God by means of the Holy Spirit. How ready are you to take on this spiritual challenge? Rate your responses to each of the following statements from 1 –5 (1 is definitely not true and 5 is definitely true). The results of this test can help indicate your present effectiveness as a follower of Christ.

Questions:

1. I am actively committed to a fellowship of men and women focused on the living Christ.
    Definitely Not True ❶ ❷ ❸ ❹ ❺ Definitely True

2. I try to persuade others to link their lives to Jesus Christ.
    Definitely Not True ❶ ❷ ❸ ❹ ❺ Definitely True

3. If the Holy Spirit were withdrawn from my life, I would notice a difference.
    Definitely Not True ❶ ❷ ❸ ❹ ❺ Definitely True

4. I know that the Holy Spirit dwells within me and I feel His presence.
    Definitely Not True ❶ ❷ ❸ ❹ ❺ Definitely True

5. I can point to a specific occasion when the Holy Spirit has worked through my life.
    Definitely Not True ❶ ❷ ❸ ❹ ❺ Definitely True

6. With the Holy Spirit's help, I know that I can dream dreams, see visions, and prophesy.
   Definitely Not True **1** **2** **3** **4** **5** Definitely True

7. When it comes to the Holy Spirit, I know the difference between dead intellectualism and Pentecost.
   Definitely Not True **1** **2** **3** **4** **5** Definitely True

8. My mind and heart are open to the presence of the Holy Spirit.
   Definitely Not True **1** **2** **3** **4** **5** Definitely True

9. I often spend time with God and ask Him for guidance.
   Definitely Not True **1** **2** **3** **4** **5** Definitely True

10. I want to make the Holy Spirit an active part of my daily life with family, friends, and co-workers.
    Definitely Not True **1** **2** **3** **4** **5** Definitely True

SCORING GUIDE

50-41:

This suggests that you already have a practical grasp of the Holy Spirit's reality and role in your life. As with even the most mature Christians, there is still room for growth and learning; however, you are being used by the Spirit in effective ways, and the outlook is great that you will become even more effective by reading books like *Halos of Fire*.

40-31:

This score suggests that you have some awareness of the Holy Spirit's reality and role in your life, but you remain shy and perhaps ambivalent about the Spirit's activity. This may be the result of limited biblical knowledge in this area. It could also be the result of peer pressure; that is, personal popularity can be more important to you than spiritual power. Or it could be the result of a weak devotional life. Spending time each day to awaken the spiritual life by praying, mediating, and reading spiritual guidebooks could help.

30 or Below:

A low score like this may indicate that you know little about the reality and role of the Holy Spirit in your life. However, this can change. In fact, as you read *Halos of Fire*, you may well experience spiritual changes that impact the way you think, feel, and act. Whether these changes occur subtly or dramatically, they will alter the way you live. For the first time, you just might discover what Jesus meant in John 10:10: "I came that they may have life, and live it abundantly."

Millions all across America and the globe are anxious for the intervention of the supernatural in their lives. They have a desperate longing to make a connection with a cosmic energy . . .

Chapter Two

Your Link to the Supernatural

When the day of Pentecost had come...
— Acts 2:1

In this chapter you will learn:

* The dual role of the head and heart when approaching God's word
* The intimate connection between Passover and Pentecost
* Why our society loves *Star Wars*
* The difference between commitment to Jesus Christ and surrender to Him

For thirty years B. H. Carroll served as pastor of the First Baptist Church in Waco, Texas. Ultimately, he became the founder and first president of the Southwestern Baptist Theological Seminary in Ft. Worth, Texas. In 1939, Carroll had this to say about the event of Pentecost as recorded in Acts 2:

> The people of God do not yet have clear conceptions of the significance of this wonderful transaction.

Indeed, if you want your mind tangled up and confused, all of its ideas reduced to thick mist and shifting shadows, you have only to read the miscellaneous literature upon the subject.[1]

What was true in the 1930s remains true some seventy years later. Interpretations of the text in Acts 2 range from fear to fantasy, doubt to delirium, ignorance to elitism. Why? The explication of these verses is usually blurred by one of two problems: dry intellectualism or raw emotionalism. Some try to understand Acts 2 by using their heads and nothing more. Others strive to understand Acts 2 by using their hearts and nothing more. However, Jesus told us that the greatest commandment in the Law is to love the Lord your God with all your heart . . . and with all your mind.

When it comes to the Bible, we are not to make a choice between the heart and the head, as if the two are in opposition to one another. Rather, the Bible is to be approached with both heart and head. The head without the heart is void of vitality, motivation, life itself. The heart without the head is void of sound judgment, discipline, and organization.

As we bring both head and heart to this passage of Scripture, I want us to start with the event that stands as the backdrop for the revolutionary outpouring of the Holy Spirit who will fill your heart, your head, and your entire life. Acts 2:1 begins, "When the day of Pentecost had come." A new and exciting era of personal empowerment began on this day, but why the day of Pentecost as opposed to some other day? Many have never considered such a question. Yet, as surely as God sent forth His Son *when the fullness of time came* (see Gal. 4:4), so God had a specific reason to fulfill His promise made through Joel on this particular day — the day of Pentecost — which refers to an event established centuries before in the Old Testament.

THE FULLNESS OF TIME

There may be several reasons why God poured forth His Spirit upon all mankind on the day of Pentecost, but I want to highlight one in particular. I believe that the outpouring of the Holy Spirit occurred at Pentecost because of the intimate connection between Passover and Pentecost.

Now, my initial reaction to this insight was a yawn too, but if you'll stay with me for a few moments I think you may be as excited about the outcome as I am. Every biblical message has to answer the "So what?" question. Anything coming to you from a pastor or teacher or writer should pass this simple test: "So what? How does what you say make a difference in my life and in the lives of those who hear it?" I believe the implied relationship between Passover and Pentecost in Acts 2:1 passes the test in resounding fashion. Here's why.

The Death Angel: Passover

Passover is the annual Hebrew festival that commemorates the tenth and final plague that fell on the nation of Egypt because Egypt's stubborn leader failed to liberate God's people, Israel, that they might worship and serve Him without restraint. In this terrible, unimaginable plague, the death angel marched through the land of Egypt taking the life of every family's firstborn child, except for those families who had painted the doorpost of their homes with the blood of a sacrificial lamb.

When the death angel saw the blood, he *passed over* that home so that the firstborn child remained alive. The blood of that sacrificial lamb, of course, symbolizes the blood of the ultimate sacrificial Lamb — Jesus Christ — who takes away the sin of all who choose to put their faith and trust in Him. As Israel was saved physically by the blood of the lamb, so we are saved spiritually by the blood of Jesus Christ. The writer of Hebrews said, "Without shedding of blood there is no forgiveness"

(9:22b). Without the shedding of Christ's blood at Calvary, there is no salvation. To be passed over in the final judgment, the sacrificial lamb is essential.

From Every Nation: Pentecost

The day following the festival of Passover, the ancient nation of Israel began seven weeks of harvest, forty-nine days of gathering the grain. On the fiftieth day following Passover, the people of Israel threw a huge party in which they celebrated the gathering of the harvest—a festival they called *Pentecost*. The word itself means *fifty*. Historians tell us that as the day of Pentecost approached, Jews from all over the known world would journey to Jerusalem. Acts 2:5 tells us that Jews were present from every nation under heaven. From all directions, long caravans of devout Israelis could be seen weaving their way to the Holy City. They carried in baskets the first fruits of the harvest as an offering to the Lord. Upon reaching the outskirts of Jerusalem, they were met by priests and Levites who escorted them into the temple itself.

As they entered the temple, they placed the baskets of grain on their shoulders, all the while singing songs of praise and adoration to God. In their songs they gave glory to God as the keeper of the harvest, the source of life-giving rain and fertile soil. Then, upon reaching the place of offering, the baskets would be given to the priests who would, in turn, set the grain before the altar of the Lord. As the grain was placed before the altar, the one bringing the gift would make a confession of thanksgiving to God by reciting the words of Deuteronomy 26:5-10:

> My father was a wandering Aramean, and he went down to Egypt and sojourned there, few in number; but there he became a great, mighty and populous nation. And the Egyptians treated us harshly and

afflicted us, and imposed hard labor on us. Then we cried to the Lord, the God of our fathers, and the Lord heard our voice and saw our affliction and our toil and our oppression; and the Lord brought us out of Egypt with a mighty hand and an outstretched arm and with great terror and with signs and wonders; and He has brought us to this place and has given us this land, a land flowing with milk and honey. Now behold, I have brought the first of the produce of the ground which You, O Lord have given me.

The Pentecostal Connection

One obvious significance of the historical Pentecost as the day of the Spirit's outpouring in Acts 2 is that those who participated in this initial outpouring were the "first fruits" of God's spiritual harvest. Among all people to receive the Spirit through the centuries to come, those gathered in this upper room were the first to be so endowed. In addition, the close connection between Passover and Pentecost says to us that we cannot enjoy the power of the Spirit unless we first accept the provision of the Savior. Without Passover there can be no Pentecost. Without the blood of the Savior there can be no baptism of the Spirit.

MAY THE TRUE FORCE BE WITH YOU

Today, untold numbers of people in this nation and across the world are seeking divine power. Millions all across America and the globe are anxious for the supernatural to intervene in their lives. They have a desperate longing to make a connection with a cosmic energy that will befriend them, protect them, guide them, enliven them, and assure them somehow of immortality.

I'm convinced that the popularity of the *Star Wars* films is due, in large part, to the concept of an invisible force that moves constantly upon the life of Luke Skywalker and others in that fictional world. Everyone can repeat the catch phrase that permeates each movie in the series: "May the force be with you," a saying almost as common as "Have a nice day." Most of all, viewers exit those movies with an overwhelming desire in their hearts to connect somehow with *The Force*. And, of course, if only you could tap into *The Force*, then death would not be an end but a beginning. The character Obewan Kinobe says to Darth Vader, "Take my life and I'll become more powerful than ever."

Channeling, karma, séances, Ouija boards, Nirvana, and transcendental meditation are all nothing more than attempts to connect personally with the supernatural. The wonderful news is that each one of us can be embraced and empowered by the supernatural. However, that connection cannot be made with the help of Obewan Kinobe or the latest swami from La-La Land. The connection can only be made through Jesus Christ, who submitted Himself on our behalf to the cruelty of the cross.

Peter boldly declared in Acts 4:12, "There is no other name under heaven that has been given among men, by which we must be saved." The apostle Paul unashamedly wrote in 1 Timothy 2:5, "There is . . . one mediator between God and men, the man Christ Jesus." There is only one who can link your life to God; there is only one who can put you in touch with the supernatural; there is only one who can bring to you a Divine Force that is not only beyond human calculation, but is so satisfying that you can lose yourself in His presence. That one is Jesus Christ, God's one-of-a-kind, unique, only begotten Son.

EAR TICKLERS AND OTHER MYTHS

So, if untold millions are looking to connect with supernatural power, and if Jesus Christ is the key to that connection, why would anyone reject Him? Why would someone turn to anyone else or anything else? Paul gives us the answer in his second letter to Timothy: "The time will come when they will not endure sound doctrine; but wanting to have their ears tickled, they will accumulate for themselves teachers in accordance with their own desires, and will turn away their ears from the truth and will turn aside to myths" (4:3-4).

Paul's words have never been more true than today, when self-gratification is the overwhelming priority, when so many make the complete and utter satisfaction of their whims and fancies their number one goal. They worship at the altar of personal inclinations and inner cravings. Does this focus on self-pleasure mean that these men and women cease striving to find a connection to divine power? Absolutely not! That deep-down hunger for the supernatural is always present, even in the lives of those who have given themselves without restraint to the party mentality or the me-first mind-set. So what do they do? Without Jesus in their lives, they seek out a connection to the divine sphere that accommodates their pleasures.

Paul says they do this in two ways. First, according to verse 3, they accumulate teachers in accordance to their own desires. They surround themselves with gurus or mentors or counselors or pundits or philosophers or mahatmas or professors who tell their followers exactly what they want to hear. The teaching of these false prophets tolerates anything, encourages everything, and demands nothing of spiritual significance.

Second, according to verse 4, these people turn away their ears from the truth and turn aside to myths. Why do they turn from the truth? What is so unattractive about the truth? Notice what Paul says in verse 2. He says that truth reproves, rebukes, and exhorts. Truth convicts us of sin, calls us to correction, and urges us to consistently engage our beliefs with our behavior. However, many are unwilling to face their sin, alter their behavior, or align their lives with eternal principles and precepts.

Therefore, they reject the truth, and in rejecting the truth they have no alternative but to align themselves with untruth, which Paul refers to in verse 4 as *myths*. Other translations use words like *folklore, fables, legends, and man-made fictions.*[2]

LIVING THE LIE OF INTELLECTUAL INTEGRITY

I've talked with numerous men and women over the years who have rejected Jesus Christ, and the reason many of them give is that of *intellectual integrity*. In reality, intellectual integrity has nothing to do with their rejection of the Savior. I say that for two reasons. First, the existence of a Creator-God is the most logical observation in the world. Anyone who looks into the beauty of nature, or witnesses the miracle of childbirth, or considers the wonders of the human body, and then denies the existence of a creator-God is mentally deficient, willfully blind, or following an agenda that denies God regardless of what one sees or experiences. However, when once a person acknowledges the existence of a Creator-God, he or she is only one short step from discovering a personal, caring God who longs to enjoy a loving relationship with them.

Second, intellectual integrity has nothing to do with their rejection of the Savior, especially when you consider the ridiculous beliefs many ultimately come to espouse. When a person rejects Jesus Christ and then accepts the foolishness of talk-show theology, that person has no intellectual integrity of any kind. The fact is they are rejecting the truth and turning aside to myths—to systems of belief that accommodate their chosen lifestyles and pleasures.

Intellectual integrity is never the real obstacle to faith in Jesus Christ. The real obstacle is the lordship of Jesus Christ. If a person accepts Jesus Christ, then that person must ultimately pattern his or her life after Jesus Christ. However, for many, patterning their lives after Jesus Christ is totally out of the question. As a result, they turn from the truth and believe a lie—and then they lie about believing the lie.

That brings us back to Pentecost. The explosive power of the Holy Spirit is available to you right now. You can connect with supernatural life today and everyday. How? By connecting with Jesus Christ. I don't mean making a commitment to Jesus. I mean surrendering to Him. When you make a commitment to Jesus, you are in control. But when you surrender to Jesus, He is in control. When you make a commitment to Jesus, that commitment is usually limited. But when you surrender to Jesus, there are no limits.

Today I am inviting you to come to Jesus Christ holding back nothing. When that happens, then your day of Pentecost will arrive — and the Holy Spirit will be all over your life.

NOTES

[1] B. H. Carroll, *The Holy Spirit*, ed. J. B. Cranfill (Nashville: Broadman Press, 1939), 31.

[2] Curtis Vaughan, ed., *The New Testament from 26 Translations* (Grand Rapids: Zondervan Bible Publishers, 1967), 1,008.

The Holy Sprit Workout #2

THE HOLY SPIRIT'S ROLE IN YOUR LIFE

Exercise 1
List three occasions when you were aware of the Holy Spirit's presence in your life.
First / Second / Third:

Exercise 2
What did those occasions have in common?

Exercise 3
What can you do to nurture those commonalities?

Exercise 4
List areas of your life that Jesus controls today.
Jesus controls:
Jesus controls:
Jesus controls:

Exercise 5
List areas of your life that you have not surrendered to Jesus.
I control:
I control:
I control:

Exercise 6
Describe what you expect to happen once you give up control of those things and surrender them to Jesus.

THE POWER FOR *L*IVING LIBRARY

PART TWO

What They Heard

Their problem was not the absence of the Holy Spirit. Their problem was ... ignorance.

Chapter Three

Like a Thousand Roaring Lions

And ... there came from heaven a noise ... and it filled the whole house...

— Acts 2:2

In this chapter you will learn:

* The when and how of receiving the Holy Spirit into your body
* The miraculous gifts brought to you by the Holy Spirit
* How the Holy Spirit can change your day-to-day living

In the summer of 1979, my wife Donna and I loaded our earthly possessions in the back of a U-Haul truck and moved with our two young sons to "the city that care forgot." There, in the metroplex of that unique southern environment, I began what would become almost nine years of formal theological training at the New Orleans Baptist Theological Seminary. For the first sixteen months of seminary life we lived in the trailer park located on the back side of the campus. Those who lived in the mobile home area had more privacy and space than those living in the seminary apartments — two of the trailer's several advantages.

One of the drawbacks, however, was the trailer park's location next to the railroad track that led east to Slidell, Louisiana, and then north to Birmingham and Atlanta. The mobile home we lived in sat only a few feet from the track, whose bed had been built up to a height just above the trailer's roof. In fact, Donna and I could lie in our bed at night, gaze out the rear window, and watch the underside of boxcars go by, sometimes at speeds up to sixty miles per hour.

We always knew when a train was coming. In the distance we could hear the whine of a locomotive approaching campus. As a train neared, its sound grew louder and louder until the noise was like the roaring of a thousand lions. As it rocketed by, the ground trembled and the trailer would literally shake on its foundation. Plates, glasses, and lamps marched across tables, pictures on the wall tilted left and right.

What I didn't know then was that God was giving me hints.

On one occasion, some good friends from Alabama came to spend a few days with us. They arrived in New Orleans well after dark and had no clue about the railroad track running just above their heads. In the wee hours of the morning one of those fast-moving trains came roaring past our trailer. We heard a panicked voice scream, "Take cover! Take cover! TORNADO!" Our friend had always heard that a tornado sounded like an oncoming train, and she knew in her heart that our mobile home was about to sprout wings and take flight.

Was it another not-so-subtle hint from above?

Acts 2 records the story of a small band of disciples gathered in an upper room somewhere in the ancient city of Jerusalem. For ten days they had been praying and focusing on the last words of the Savior. For ten days they had been longing to receive what had been promised by the Father and proclaimed by the Son: the outpouring of God's Spirit that would immerse them in the exciting sphere of the Holy Spirit. Just as Jesus had been with them, so the Spirit would be with them. Just as Jesus had been empowered, so they would be empowered. Just as Jesus had operated by the anointing of God, so they would operate by the anointing of God.

But when would that anointing come? How would they know that the anointing had come? What would the experience truly mean to them? As we have seen, the answer to the question "when" is found in Acts 2:1, "When the day of Pentecost had come..." The answer to "how" is in the very next verse, "And suddenly there came from heaven a noise like a violent rushing wind, and it filled the whole house where they were sitting."

Have you ever tried to imagine this experience, to capture the electricity of this moment? I've often heard people say that when they get to Heaven they are going to ask God some particular question that mystifies them now. Some say they will ask for explanations of events in their lives that seemed to have no answer. The truth is, we will probably be like Job who desperately wanted to call God into account concerning the circumstances that had overtaken his life, but when the opportunity finally came for an audience with God, Job found himself unable to speak. Being in the presence of God will most likely answer all of our questions without a word being spoken.

But just in case I can talk, I'm going to ask God to re-create the outpouring of His Spirit in that upper room and allow me to be a participant. I want to hear, firsthand, the noise like a violent rushing wind as it filled that room. Will it sound like one of those Birmingham-bound trains pounding steel at sixty miles per hour a few feet above my head? Will I think a tornado is about to tear off the roof? Will I hear the roar of a thousand lions? I want to hear that noise in heaven, not in a trailer. I want to see, from an eyewitness perspective, those flames as they rested on the men and women who were present. I want to know, experientially, what it is like to speak in a language I've never studied and be able to communicate instantaneously with someone of a different nationality.

GOD'S CORONATION TRUMPETS

This marvelous scene, as recorded in Acts 2:2-4, will no more occur again than will the birth of Jesus Christ. His birth is an historical event never to happen again, and so is the *initial* outpouring of the Spirit. What the Scripture records in verses 2 and 3, Scripture never records again. What the Scripture depicts in verse 4 is depicted only twice more, and when we study verse 4 in detail we learn the vital theological significance of those occurrences. The noise, the fire, and the tongues are coronation trumpets announcing the genesis of a new and exciting era among the people of God, an era in which all of His disciples—without exception—are to be immersed into the sphere of the Holy Spirit.

If the scene is not to be recreated, why even consider the passage? For the same reason we consider any biblical passage. The historical elements of a particular text may be frozen in the past, but the truth and power that springs forth from it are beyond time and season. The opening verses of Acts 2 introduce us to the Holy Spirit's character and nature. There we learn two key principles about the Holy Spirit and our relationship to Him.

Principle 1: We Receive the Holy Spirit at Conversion.

All who receive Jesus Christ simultaneously receive the Holy Spirit. This sudden gift is the central notion of Acts 2:1: "And suddenly there came a noise from heaven...." These followers of Christ were baptized with the Holy Spirit just as Jesus proclaimed in Acts 1:5 and just as God had promised through the Old Testament prophet, Joel. They are, in this moment, enveloped by the presence of the Holy Spirit. Since that Pentecost, all who accept Jesus Christ also receive—in that moment—the Holy Spirit as an intimate companion.

Principle 2: Repentance Opens the Door to the Holy Spirit.

Acts 2:38-39 says, "Repent, and each of you be baptized in the name of Jesus Christ for the forgiveness of your sins; and you shall receive the gift of the Holy Spirit. For the promise is for you and your children and for all who are far off, as many as the Lord our God shall call to Himself." We could get bogged down in controversial debate over verse 38, and believe me, I love to debate. But let me offer a paraphrase of these two verses that will tell you briefly what I think they mean: Repentance, as symbolically expressed by water baptism, is the key to the forgiveness of sins and the gift of the Holy Spirit – a gift promised to you and to your children and to all who, in the centuries to come, respond to the call of God for salvation in Jesus Christ.

Acts 3:19 supports this interpretation: "Repent and return, that your sins may be wiped away, in order that times of refreshing may come from the presence of the Lord." According to Acts 3:19, when we repent, our sins are wiped away and times of refreshing come. Repentance results in the forgiveness of sin and the reception of the Holy Spirit.

First Corinthians 12:13 says, "By one Spirit we were all baptized into one body ... and we were all made to drink of one Spirit." In other words, Paul is saying, You are in the body of Christ, each one of you, because you have been enveloped — immersed, surrounded, baptized — with the Holy Spirit. Some believers in the Corinthian church claimed that if a person did not have a certain spiritual gift or a particular spiritual ability, then he or she did not have the Holy Spirit. Paul responded by saying: To the contrary, all of you, as followers of Christ, have been overshadowed by the Holy Spirit; you have all received the Holy Spirit into your life.

Galatians 3:2-3 asks, "Did you receive the Spirit by the works of the Law, or by hearing with faith? Are you so foolish? Having begun by the Spirit, are you now being perfected by the flesh?"

Paul is being very clear: You received the Holy Spirit not because you earned or deserved His presence but because you heard the good news about Jesus Christ and staked your life on Him. When you began your life as a follower of Christ, you began by means of the Holy Spirit.

Likewise, Romans 8:9b says, "If anyone does not have the Spirit of Christ, he does not belong to Him." That is, if the Holy Spirit is not in your life, you cannot possibly be a Christian. Said another way, if you are a Christian, then the Holy Spirit has surely invaded your life.

IGNORANCE IS FAR FROM BLISS

We acquire the Spirit of God through the Son of God. Every person who has trusted Christ as Savior and Lord has been baptized or immersed into the sphere of the Holy Spirit—at that instant. Some of you may be asking yourself: So what? Why is this man writing on a topic as simple as this? Why doesn't he talk about something that is deep, something that is not so elemental? Because I've discovered again and again that a huge number of Christians have no idea about the Holy Spirit. Through the years, I've seen multitudes of men and women who were born again but remained totally unaware of the Holy Spirit as an ever-present companion and vital resource for living.

How can that be? Well, ignorance of the Holy Spirit is no more unusual for Christians than the ignorance many people have of the abilities present within them from the moment of conception. Only through training, experience, and the encouragement of others do those native abilities begin to spring forth. The same is true for spiritual growth: It isn't automatic, but is predicated upon spiritual instruction and personal commitment.

Paul knew this about the Corinthians. In writing to the church at Corinth, Paul asked them in 1 Corinthians 6:19:

"Do you not know that your body is a temple of the Holy Spirit who is in you, whom you have from God?" That is, Do you not know that your body is a sanctuary of the Holy Spirit? Do you not know that your body is inhabited by the Holy Spirit? Do you not know that your body is the dwelling place of the Holy Spirit? Do you not know that your body houses the Holy Spirit who has been sent to you as a gift from God?

Their problem was not the absence of the Holy Spirit. Their problem was ignorance about the presence and person and power of the Holy Spirit. They had little or no comprehension of the Spirit. Perhaps some of the Christians at Corinth had never even considered the Spirit. But their difficulty was not an inability to know. They had never been taught to know.

HOW THE HOLY SPIRIT CAN CHANGE YOUR DAILY LIFE

Let me ask you a personal question: Did *you* know your body is inhabited by the Holy Spirit? Have you grasped that reality? Better yet, have you been grasped by that reality? What happens when you come to the understanding that the Holy Spirit has literally taken up residence in your body?

First, every day of life and every place you are take on greater significance. You no longer view God as *out there*, but *right here*. One of the most colorful characters in the book of Genesis is Jacob. On one particular journey through the wilderness he made the marvelous discovery that God was with him even in the desert. He said: Surely the Lord is in this place, and I did not know it ... How awesome is this place! This is none other than the house of God, and this is the gate of heaven (see Gen. 28:16-17). When you come to see that the Holy Spirit resides in your body, you begin to realize that every place is a holy place, that every place is the house of God — the very gate of heaven. That means that where you are, God is, and where God is, God is active.

Second, you will find yourself in an ongoing conversation with God. Your day will be dotted by abbreviated conversations with God as you constantly take issues and questions and situations to the Lord. I don't mean that you never think about anything else or that you will be so distracted you fail to take care of business. Rather, you will know God is resident and can be called upon and relied upon immediately. A good friend in Alabama tells me that she throws prayer darts to God all day long; that is, she seeks His guidance and wisdom and power at needful moments throughout the day. Of course, these abbreviated moments ultimately lead to lingering interludes of extended length — not out of force or habit, but out of a sense of intimate companionship.

Third, you will become more careful about where your body goes and what your body does. In his first letter to the Corinthian church, Paul wrote:

> Food is for the stomach, and the stomach is for food; but God will do away with both of them. Yet the body is not for immorality, but for the Lord; and the Lord is for the body... Do you not know that your bodies are members of Christ? Shall I then take away the members of Christ and make them members of a harlot? May it never be! ... Do you not know that your body is a temple of the Holy Spirit? ... For you have been bought with a price; therefore glorify God in your body (6:13,15,19-20).

Paul is saying that the presence of the Holy Spirit makes the body much more than a biological machine driven from one meal to the next, from one sexual encounter to the next. He is telling us that our physical bodies belong not to us but to God as instruments by which we serve and glorify Him. Most of all,

Paul is telling us that the presence of the Holy Spirit deeply affects our behavior and conduct.

"PREACHER'S COMING — HIDE THE WHISKEY!"

I often notice that people change their behavior when they become aware of my presence. They see me as a representative of God. I don't have to say a word; my mere presence reminds them that God makes a difference in the way they behave. When I leave, they mistakenly think God leaves, and their behavior changes again.

In one of my Louisiana pastorates, I stopped by unannounced to see a man and woman who had been long-time members of the church. As I entered the carport, I discovered the door to the house open, and I heard lots of guests inside. So I walked in without knocking. Someone saw me coming down the hall and shouted loudly, "Hello, preacher!" I then heard people scrambling around and bottles clanking. As I turned the corner into the kitchen, several folks were in a panic trying to get the whiskey glasses off the table and into the sink.

What did their actions reveal? They had no idea about the presence of the Holy Spirit in their lives. When you are aware that the Holy Spirit actually and literally lives in your body, you don't need the presence of a pastor to keep your body and behavior in check. Many of us involve ourselves in various activities simply because we do not live in the reality of the Holy Spirit's presence. The Holy Spirit is not merely a representative of God; rather, the Holy Spirit is God.

"I AIN'T NOBODY'S NOTHING"

When a person comes to the understanding that the Holy Spirit resides in his or her body, that person's self-esteem and sense of personal value is raised astronomically. During World War II, following a particularly heavy night of bombing raids on

London, a pastor began searching through the rubble and debris hoping to find survivors. At one point he heard someone crying. As he turned, he saw a young boy sitting on what was left of the front steps where a home had been. The pastor tried to offer comfort, but the boy's sobbing continued as though his heart would break. When the crying stopped, the preacher asked, "Son, whose boy are you?" Then the crying started all over again. Eventually, the boy answered, "Mister, I ain't nobody's nothing." The pastor learned later that the boy's father had been killed in battle, that his mother and sister had died in the bombings, and that he was all alone.[1]

Like that boy, you may think you've lost everything and have nothing to offer. You may think you are absolutely useless. Yet, if the Holy Spirit inhabits your life, you are anything but nobody's nothing.

God has counted you so worthy that He moved into your body. God has loved you so much that He has taken up residence in your life—literally and actually. You are an instrument in the hands of God, anywhere and everywhere. You are His and He is yours.

Revel in the intimacy He brings to your life.

Enjoy the purpose He gives to every circumstance.

NOTE

[1] Landrum Leavell, II, *The Doctrine of the Holy Spirit* (Nashville: Convention Press, 1983), 52-53.

The Holy Spirit Workout #3

RECONNECTION ROUTINE

Exercise 1

Can you remember a time when you felt particularly in touch with the Holy Spirit within you? Close your eyes and try to rehearse that moment mentally with as much detail as you can. Now, quickly write down the first five words that come to your mind to describe that experience. Were you breathless? Excited? Overwhelmed? Curious? At peace? Bold? Confident?

Your five words:
1.   2.   3.   4.   5.

What do these words reveal to you about the nature and character of the Holy Spirit?

Exercise 2

The next time you are working, whether at home or at the office, and you encounter a difficulty—stop everything. Close your eyes and speak to God. Explain the problem and what you are feeling. Ask for His guidance, comfort, and power. Then, when you have a chance to return to this book, answer the following:

1. How difficult was it for you to utter those first words, aloud or silently?
2. How did speaking to God affect your mood?
3. How did the conversation affect the problem's outcome?

The Holy Spirit comes upon us with force. The Holy Spirit comes upon us mightily. And when He does, we receive supernatural abilities we never had before.

Chapter Four

The Gifts Within

To each one is given the manifestation the Spirit...
– 1 Corinthians 12:7

In this chapter you will learn:

* The Scripture's foundational principle for the Holy Spirit's impact on personal living
* Possible gifts of the Holy Spirit
* The ministries and effects that we can manifest through the Holy Spirit
* How to find increasing confidence in serving the Lord

The Holy Spirit is God's marvelous gift to every person who places the reigns of their lives in the hands of Jesus Christ. Without the delay of a single second, the Holy Spirit—who is God Himself—literally and actually takes up residence in the body of the person who accepts the death and resurrection of Jesus Christ as his or her own.

We learn from the book of Acts that the Holy Spirit comes upon the believer instantaneously. The book of Acts also teaches that the Holy Spirit comes upon the believer mightily: "And suddenly there came from heaven a noise like a violent, rushing wind." Luke, the author of Acts, is telling us that the Holy Spirit brings to our lives a divine energy, a heavenly force that enables us to do what we could not do before. Most of all, the Holy Spirit brings to every believer abilities that can be used in powerful and exciting ways for God.

WE ARE NOT ALONE

In the book of Genesis, Joseph became successful in Potiphar's house because "the Lord was with Joseph" (39:2). How was the Lord with him? By means of the Holy Spirit, who inhabited his life. Joseph later became successful even while in prison (on false charges) because "the Lord was with Joseph" (39:21). How was the Lord with Him? By means of the Holy Spirit. Still later, Joseph became successful in the palace of Egypt because, as the Pharaoh explicitly stated, he was a man in whom dwelled a divine spirit (41:38), that is the Holy Spirit. The Holy Spirit dwelled in Joseph's body and enabled him to do and accomplish extraordinary things — things he could never have done otherwise.

The book of Exodus introduces us to a man named Bezalel, a man who was "filled ... with the Spirit of God in wisdom, in understanding, in knowledge, and in all kinds of craftsmanship, to make artistic designs ... in the cutting of stones ... and in the carving of wood, that he [could] work in all kinds of craftsmanship" (31:2-5). Bezalel, by means of the Holy Spirit, could do what he had not been able to do on his own.

Consider Moses. He was being crushed by the pressing throngs of people who constantly sought him for help. He cried out to God, "I alone am not able to carry all this people, because it is too burdensome for me" (Num. 11:14). God answered, "Gather for Me seventy men ... and bring them to the tent of meeting, and let them take their stand there with you. Then I will come down ... and I will take of the Spirit who is upon you, and will put Him upon them; and they shall bear the burden of the people with you" (Num. 11:16-17). The Holy Spirit took up residence in the lives of those seventy men and they were then able to do what they had not been able to do before.

You've probably heard the Old Testament story of Gideon, who with three hundred men overtook and defeated an army that numbered in the tens of thousands. How did he accomplish that feat? Judges 6:34 says, "The Spirit of the Lord came upon Gideon."

Samson slew a young lion with his bare hands. How did he do it? Judges 14:6 says, "The Spirit of the Lord came upon him mightily." Samson single-handedly took the lives of thirty men at once. How did he do it? Judges 14:19 says, "The Spirit of the Lord came upon him mightily." Samson killed a thousand of the enemy with the jawbone of a donkey. How did he do it? Judges 15:14 says, "The Spirit of the Lord came upon him mightily."

When Samuel anointed Saul as Israel's first king, he said, "The Spirit of the Lord will come upon you mightily and you shall ... be changed into another man ... Do ... what the occasion requires, for God is with you" (1 Sam. 10:6-7).

When Samuel anointed David as Israel's second king, the Bible says, The Spirit of the Lord came mightily upon David from that day forward (1 Sam. 16:13). One chapter later, young David defeated the giant Goliath. As we know, he made many other spectacular conquests through the course of his life. How did he do it? By means of the Holy Spirit.

This is a foundational teaching of Scripture from beginning to end: *The Holy Spirit comes upon us with force. The Holy Spirit comes upon us mightily. When He does, we receive capabilities we never had before.*

IT'S THE HOW THAT COUNTS

Did you know that everything Jesus did He did by means of the Holy Spirit? When Jesus began His public ministry, the Bible says that "the Holy Spirit descended upon Him in bodily form like a dove" (Luke 3:22).

Luke 4:1 says, "Jesus, full of the Holy Spirit, returned from the Jordan and was led around by the Spirit in the wilderness for forty days."

Luke 4:14 says, "Jesus returned to Galilee in the power of the Spirit."

Luke 4:18 tells us that as Jesus taught in the synagogue in Nazareth, He said, "The Spirit of the Lord is upon Me ... to preach the gospel to the poor.... to proclaim release to the captives, and recovery of sight to the blind, to set free those who are oppressed, to proclaim the favorable year of the Lord."

Many interpreters, in commenting on the words that Christ spoke in Nazareth, talk about the *what* of Christ's ministry but not the *how*. Yet, the Bible is concerned as much with the *how* as the *what*. In Matthew 12:28, Jesus not only said "I cast out demons," but, "I cast out demons by the Spirit of God." In His earthly life Jesus did everything by the presence and power of the Holy Spirit, and He promised His followers that He would send to each of them the presence and power of the Holy Spirit so that they might live as He lived.

I want you to understand that the Holy Spirit is not merely a phenomenon of the ancient past, some shadowy netherworld figure who roamed the pages of mythological fables. I want you to be grasped by the truth that the Holy Spirit is as real as Jesus Christ because the Holy Spirit is Jesus Christ. I want you to be struck with the life-changing theology that the Holy Spirit is as powerful as God because the Holy Spirit is God. That is important because the Bible teaches us that the Holy Spirit is literally present in the here and now with all who have put their faith and trust in Jesus Christ and that His presence enables every believer to serve God forcefully and effectively.

I'm not saying that you will be able to interpret dreams as did Joseph or wake up tomorrow and be a skilled artisan in the fashion of Bezalel. I am not saying that you will have the physical strength and power to kill a lion with your bare hands or be able to open the eyes of the blind and unstop the ears of the deaf. However, I am saying that as a disciple of Jesus Christ, the Holy Spirit has come upon you and He has come upon you mightily. I am saying that because of the Holy Spirit's presence in your life, you now have abilities that you did not have before. Moreover, you can now use those abilities to do and accomplish things you could never do and accomplish before.

VARIETIES OF GIFTS, MINISTRIES, AND EFFECTS

First Corinthians 12:7 says, "To each one is given the manifestation of the Spirit." This verse tells us that the Holy Spirit manifests Himself in a special way through the life of each and every believer. No one has been left out. No one has been overlooked. Not one Christian has been neglected. The Holy Spirit has come upon each of us, and His presence can be seen at work in forceful, powerful ways. How is the Holy Spirit manifested in our lives? 1 Corinthians 12:4-6 gives the answer: "Now there are *varieties of gifts*, but the same Spirit. And *there are varieties of ministries*, and the same Lord. *There are varieties of effects*, but the same God who works all things in all persons" (emphasis mine). Let's examine each of these.

What Are Your Gifts?

Paul tells us that the Holy Spirit is manifested in our lives through the particular "gift" or "gifts" that He brings to us as individuals. Paul is referring to a supernatural ability that is given to us in conjunction with the presence of the Holy Spirit, a supernatural ability whereby a person serves the Kingdom of God and performs certain tasks on God's behalf.

Understand that not every Christian receives the same gift or abilities, but every Christian — without exception — receives at least one gift or ability. Paul says in verse 4, "there are a variety of gifts…" That is, there are numerous gifts or abilities that are available from God, and when the Holy Spirit comes into a person's life, He brings with Him one or more of those gifts or abilities that become a vital and meaningful part of life.

1. Your gift or ability may be *faith*.
   You may be one of those valiant Christians who pushes forward when confronted by impenetrable obstacles and formidable circumstances; the kind of person who dreams the undreamable, believes the unbelievable, and expects the unexpected; the kind of person who tears down mountains in one place and builds them in another (Rom. 12:6).

2. You may have the gift or ability of *teaching*.
   You are able to communicate biblical truth so that others can see how the Word of God intersects with the everyday affairs of their lives (Rom. 12:7).

3. Your gift or ability may be *serving*.
   You have the uncanny ability to see needs in a particular area, and you move into action by developing a way to meet that need (Rom 12:7).

4. Your gift or ability may be *helping*.
   You are amazing when it comes to rolling up your sleeves and assisting others in getting some job or task completed.

This may not sound impressive, but it's a supernatural ability (1 Pet. 4:10-11).

5. Your gifts or abilities may be *mercy* and *encouragement.* You are not only moved to sympathy by the hurts and pains of others, but you are moved to action on their behalf. You can put your arm around someone who is distressed, discouraged, in despair and offer such inspiration that the person is lifted out of that defeated attitude and placed once more on the road to success or victory (Rom. 12:8).

6. Your gift or ability may be *giving.* You are one of those Christians who goes far beyond the tithe. Rather than stopping at 10 percent, you draw joyfully and freely from your own resources to help meet financial or material needs within the body of Christ—and you do so as a habit of life (Rom. 12:8).

7. Your gift or ability may be *leadership.* You have an astounding capacity to champion a cause, to communicate goals and visions, to persuade and motivate others to follow a course of action.

8. You gift or ability may be *administrating.* You are like the helmsman who keeps the ship on course and efficiently tends to the ongoing details of the church or a particular arm of the church (1 Cor. 12:28).

9. You may have the ability to *distinguish spirits.* You can accurately discern the real motivation behind an action, an attitude, an idea, or a personality. You may even be able to discern troubled hearts and lives

although those hearts and lives be a thousand miles re-moved from your location (1 Cor. 12:10).

10. You may have the gift of evangelist.
    Might you have an amazing ability to present the good news of Jesus Christ to others and bring them to a point of decision? (Eph. 4: 8-12).

I don't know how you have been gifted, but there is no doubt that every Christian—no exceptions — has at least one super-natural gift or ability. You may have a blend of several gifts. You may have a minor gift as well as a major gift — but every Christian has at least one gift, at least one ability that works through them in forceful, effective ways.

What Are Your Ministries?

Paul also reveals that the Holy Spirit operates forcefully in our lives through a particular ministry or ministries brought to us (1 Cor. 12:5). A ministry is an opportunity for service. Where-as a gift refers to a specified ability, a ministry is the unique way in which that ability is used or employed. Knowing your spiri-tual gift is not enough. You must also know your ministry, that is, the way in which God wants you to use the ability He has placed in your care.

For instance, you may have the gift of teaching, but how is that gift to be employed? Some people are wonderful at com-municating biblical truth to adults, but put them in front of teenagers and they fail miserably. Some people may perform well in small group settings or one-on-one encounters, but send them out to address a huge crowd and they crumble.

You may have the gift of leadership, but is your gift of lead-ership geared toward adults, teenagers, or children? You may be a marvelous administrator, but is your ministry to the church at large or to a more narrowly defined part of the church? You may have the gift of evangelism, but the practical way in which your gift is used may be to intellectuals in the fashion of C. S. Lewis, or to prison inmates in the manner of Charles Colson, or to some other particular group of people.

Paul is telling us that we are all specialists. Each Christian is uniquely equipped to meet a different need and challenge, and once you determine the gift or gifts the Holy Spirit has brought to your life and you fling yourself into the appropriate opportunity for service, the force of the Holy Spirit will be seen through you in undeniable ways.

What Are Your Effects?

First Corinthians 12:6 says, "There are varieties of effects." Paul is also telling us that the Holy Spirit is manifested in our lives through *effects*, a translation of a word that refers to energy and to results. Some gifts and ministries are high-powered while other gifts and ministries are low-key. Some are fast-paced while others are laid back. Some are attention-grabbing while others are subtle and quiet. Some gifts and ministries erect the buildings while other gifts and ministries build the saints. Some gifts and ministries are far-reaching while others are near-reaching.

I may not be the preacher Charles Stanley is, nor the visionary Jerry Vines is. I may not be the administrator Jim Henry is, nor the theologian W. A. Criswell was. And I know that I'm not the evangelist Billy Graham is. But verse 6 also promises: "God works all things in all persons." I am what I am by the grace of God. I will never be anybody else, nor do I need to be anybody else, nor should I try to be anybody else. God has energized my gifts and ministries in ways that are pleasing to Him. Most of all, verse 6 means that whatever wonderful, marvelous things take place in the church I serve are to be credited, not to this pastor, but to God, from whose hands alone flow all effects.

Paul understood this well. Among the numerous problems faced by the church at Corinth was a division within the congregation over leadership. Some said: We follow Paul. Others said: We follow Apollos. Still others said: We follow Peter. Paul responded to that schismatic thinking like this: "What ... is Apollos? And what is Paul? Servants through whom you believed, even as the Lord gave opportunity to each one. I planted, Apollos watered, but God was causing the growth. So then neither the one who plants nor the one who waters is anything, but God who causes the growth ... Let no one boast in men ... whether Paul or Apollos or Cephas ... you belong to Christ" (1 Cor. 3:5-7, 21-23).

God gives the gifts. God gives the ministries. And only God gets credit for the results.

INCREASING JOY, INCREASING CONFIDENCE

If you are a disciple of Jesus Christ, the Holy Spirit not only resides in your body, but He is a great stirring force. He has given you at least one ability to be used in marvelous ways. When you allow that truth to lay claim upon your heart, and when you discover the ability or abilities that have been showered upon your life, then your relationship to God will take on at least two new dimensions. First, you will find increasing joy in serving Him because you will stop doing what you have not been gifted to do, and you will start prioritizing the abilities that God has placed in your life. Many Christians are miserable in serving God because they are attempting to do what they have not been fitted to do. Likewise, many Christians are miserable in their relationship with God because they are not serving Him at all. Joy is not found in sitting but in serving. Knowing your gifts and ministries compels you to action, and action—springing forth from God's special design for your life—results in satisfaction.

Finally, when you discover the ability or abilities that have been showered upon your life, you will find increasing confidence in serving the Lord. When you know that the Holy Spirit has come upon you mightily, you not only tend to be more bold in stepping forward to serve, but you develop an attitude of expectancy in the process of serving. You start looking for reasons to succeed rather than fail.

When that happens, no one will have any doubt that the Holy Spirit is God forcefully at work in your life and through it.

The Holy Spirit Workout #4

REFINING THE GIFTS OF THE HOLY SPIRIT

Exercise 1
This chapter discusses possible abilities or gifts dwelling within you, courtesy of the Holy Spirit. The gifts of:
- faith
- teaching
- serving
- helping
- mercy
- encouragement
- giving
- leadership
- administering
- distinguishing spirits
- evangelizing

Which of these gifts do you feel most connected to? What experiences have helped you to recognize these gifts of the Holy Spirit within you? What other gifts do you have that aren't on the above list?

Exercise 2
A *ministry* in this chapter is defined as an opportunity for service, the way in which God wants you to use the ability He has placed in your care.

Using the gifts you listed in exercise 1, choose at least two and write down the current opportunities you have for using them:

Opportunities for Gift #1:

Opportunities for Gift #2:

Exercise 3
Get to Know Your Effects

As you contemplate your gifts and opportunities for using them, take a moment to imagine the outcomes. What do you want to see happen? How do you hope that your efforts will change the lives of others or the life of your church? Complete this sentence:

Using my gifts, I want to:

Many of you could stand today and give testimony to the great personal struggles you have encountered. They may be private struggles; they may be fierce wrestling matches within the secret places of your heart. No one else may know about them. But they are real — to you and to God.

Chapter Five

Collisions
of the Heart

*For the flesh sets its desire against the Spirit, and the Spirit sets
its desire against the flesh...*
– Galatians 5:17

What you will learn in this chapter:
* The Holy Spirit's desire for totality
* Why the struggle between flesh and Spirit is important
  for Christians
* The very worst thing that could happen to any Christian
* Three steps Christians can take to win the battle of the
  flesh

If I asked you to name the four most important events in Christian history, how would you answer? For me, the four most important events in Christian history are the Incarnation, the Crucifixion, the Resurrection, and Pentecost. The Incarnation, because that is the day God put on skin and became a man. The Crucifixion, because that is the day God, who put on flesh in the person of Jesus Christ, took upon His shoulders the sins of the entire world for all ages and made atonement for those sins. The Resurrection, because that is the day God defeated death forever. Pentecost, because that is the day God initiated the explosive new era in which He would immerse into the realm of the Holy Spirit all who would stake their lives upon the Incarnation, the Crucifixion, and the Resurrection.

If you have surrendered your life to the Lord Jesus Christ, then you have received into your life, literally and actually, the gift of the Holy Spirit. In conjunction with turning your heart toward Christ, the Holy Spirit has taken up residence in your body. This moment, because you are a disciple of Jesus Christ, the Holy Spirit—who is not merely a representative of God but who is God Himself—has moved into the command-and-control center of your life.

As we have learned, that event took place instantaneously and mightily. The Holy Spirit not only came upon you suddenly, as in the blink of an eye, the Holy Spirit also came upon you with great force, giving you at least one supernatural gift or ability, at least one divinely ordained ministry or avenue of service, and a wonderful measure of extraordinary energy that makes you effective on His behalf.

ROOMS FULL OF SPIRIT

Although Acts 2:2 tells us that the Holy Spirit comes upon us instantaneously and mightily, it also tells us that the Holy Spirit comes upon us pervasively: "And suddenly there came from heaven a noise like a violent rushing wind, and it filled the whole house where they were sitting." Take note of the phrase, *and it filled the whole house*. The word translated *filled* refers to a force that dominates and controls the object that has been filled—in this case, the entire house. The idea is that of totality.

What is Luke telling us about the Holy Spirit? When a person is immersed into the world of the Holy Spirit, the Holy Spirit impacts every facet of his or her life. Not a single room, so to speak, is left untouched. One error many Christians make is to compartmentalize their existence. That is, they attempt to separate the different aspects of their lives so that each individual area is unrelated and disconnected to all the rest. Some strive to differentiate between private life and public life, as if the two are completely disassociated.

In the 1992 presidential campaign, for example, there were those who, in an effort to overcome the many objections to the character flaws of one candidate in particular, said that character should never be an issue in a political campaign. We were asked to believe that what a man did in his personal life in no way affected what he did in his public life. People said that because a man could not be trusted to do right by his family in no way implied that he would not do right by his nation. They were wrong, tragically so.

In the same way, there are those within Christian circles who attempt to separate their spiritual beliefs from every other aspect of their lives. They've got their spiritual life in one place, their business life in another, their recreational life off to one side, and their family life off to another. They think what happens in one area has no connection to what happens in another. What they read in the Bible has no impact on how they conduct their business, and to think that it should is preposterous, according to them. What they are taught on Sunday has no bearing on anything that takes place Monday through Saturday, and to think it should is unreasonable. Sound familiar?

However, the Holy Spirit invades every aspect of a person's life. God is not looking to be placed on the mantle like a trophy that is dusted and polished when guests stop by for a visit. He does not want a single room of your life while every other room remains off-limits. Rather, the Holy Spirit has come to you that He might take the leadership role in every phase of your existence, without exception.

THE SECRET PLACES OF YOUR CONSCIENCE

If the Holy Spirit wants to take the lead position in our lives, how does He do it? One of the ways is by affecting the believer's conscience. Notice what Jesus said to His disciples in John 16:8: "He [the Holy Spirit], when He comes, will convict the world concerning sin and righteousness and judgment." The word translated *convict* is a legal term that refers to a cross-examination for the purpose of convincing or refuting an opponent. Jesus is telling us that, by means of the Holy Spirit, God challenges a person's thought processes so that he or she knows what is right and wrong, and knows — whether they admit it or not — they will be called into account.

This specific action of the Holy Spirit as outlined in John 16:8 is, of course, addressed to the Spirit's work in the lives of those without Christ. However, the convincing/convicting work of the Holy Spirit does not stop with those who have never established a personal relationship with the Lord. Once a person becomes a Christian and the Holy Spirit takes up residence in that person's life, he or she must then contend with what can be strong inner prompting and challenges produced by the Holy Spirit. In fact, many of us could stand today and give testimony to the great personal struggles we have encountered due to the presence of the Holy Spirit. They may be private struggles; they may be wrestling matches within the secret places of your conscience; no one else may know about them, but they are real.

THE ENGINE OF DESIRE

Galatians 5:17 says, "For the flesh sets its desire against the Spirit, and the Spirit sets its desire against the flesh; for these are in opposition to one another, so that you may not do the things that you please." Becoming a Christian does not do away with the desires of the flesh. When Paul uses the word *flesh*, he is talking about that element within each of us that wants to live life apart from God. The flesh is Self in charge. The flesh is Self on the throne. The flesh is Self occupying the command-and-control center of our decision-making processes. The word translated *desire* refers to inner cravings and longings. Thus the phrase *desire of the flesh* depicts our innermost yearnings as those yearnings drive us toward gratification of Self. The desire of the flesh urges us and pushes us to live life in utter disregard of anyone but Self.

This is exactly what happened to Eve in the garden. Genesis 3:6 says, "When (she) saw that the tree was good for food, and that it was a delight to the eyes, and that the tree was desirable to make one wise, she took from its fruit and ate." In total disregard of God and of the consequences, Eve reached out and took hold of that which her inner cravings and longings told her would bring personal satisfaction and pleasure.

Is our problem not the same as Eve's? Why the addictions? Why the adulteries? Why the murders? Why the rapes? Why the hatred? Why the pornography? Why the alcohol? Why the robbery? Why the division? Because we are all driven from within to satisfy our cravings and longings. Have you ever heard someone say: "There are no moral absolutes, and no one can tell me what is right and what is wrong"? Here is what that person is really saying: "I want to be in charge of my own life, and I want to give vent to every craving and desire of my heart without restraint, if I so choose."

HEARTS OF STONE

Becoming a Christian does not do away with the desires of the flesh. That is important to know, especially for a new believer. The day comes when the initial tide of spiritual excitement ebbs and this new believer discovers that the pre-Christian life, with all of its inclinations, is still rumbling around in the heart. That discovery can be such a shock that a new believer can be thrown into doubt and confusion about the reality of his or her relationship with Jesus Christ. Or, the reappearance of those old drives can cause them to conclude that the Christian experience is a false experience and they give up altogether.

But Galatians 5:17 also teaches us that, as Christians, we have a divine Companion who does battle on our behalf with the desires of the flesh. You and I alone — without the help of God — are outmatched against the desires of the flesh. So God has placed the Holy Spirit within us to act as an opponent to the flesh and its desires. That is why you find yourself, from time to time, engulfed in a huge struggle of the heart.

There are those who mistakenly worry when Christians struggle over the do's and don'ts of life. Yet I am not nearly as concerned about those who are struggling as I am about those who say they have no struggle at all. If you have no struggle with the do's and don'ts of life, then one of three things is true for you:

- You have no struggle because you have so mastered the Christian walk that your flesh is completely hog-tied. Now, if you've reached that level I want to find out how you did it, because I've certainly not done it and I've yet to meet a person who has.

- You have no struggle because there is no spiritual life in you. You have rejected Jesus Christ so often and so completely that your heart has hardened to the point that you can no longer tell the difference between right and wrong. Or, if you can tell the difference, you simply don't care.

- You have no struggle because—even though you are a Christian—you have rebuffed the prompting of the Holy Spirit for such an extended period of time that the Holy Spirit is no longer confronting you. Instead, as Paul wrote, you have quenched the Spirit completely (1 Thess. 5:19) or perhaps you have been "delivered to Satan for the destruction of the flesh" (1 Cor. 5:5).

THE VERY WORST THING

Not everyone struggles with the same issues, but we all struggle. If you are not struggling with the do's and don'ts of life, at least in some measure, you may be walking and living on dangerously thin ice. Be glad for the inner struggle of the conscience. That struggle is a sign of spiritual life. Even so, I know some Christians who long to be free of the struggle so they can live their lives as they please without interference from inner restraint.

As you were growing up, did you ever badger your parents about letting you do something that you knew they didn't want you to do? Did you badger them so much that they finally threw their hands up in despair and said, "I've had it! Do whatever you want to do. Just don't come to me anymore. I'm tired of arguing about it!" Did you know the worst thing that could happen to any child is for a parent to say those words and really mean them? I've said those words to my children, but I never meant them, and they knew I didn't mean them. The worst thing I could have done to one of my teenaged children would have been to remove all restraint, to step out of the way and allow them to do anything and everything they wanted to do.

The worst thing that can happen to any Christian is to lose that sense of struggle. If the Holy Spirit steps out of the way and gives complete freedom to do anything and everything you want to do, there is nothing left but annihilation and destruction. That is true for a nation, for your family, and for you as an individual.

THE DEVIL AND DIRTY OLD MEN

Galatians 5:17 also teaches us that the flesh fights back. The flesh doesn't lay down and die when the Holy Spirit comes on the scene. The flesh doesn't roll over and play dead when the Holy Spirit flexes His muscles. If the Holy Spirit is opposed to the flesh, the flesh is opposed to the Holy Spirit. If the Spirit is determined to dominate the flesh, the flesh is determined to dominate the Spirit.

The flesh will attempt to foil the desires of the Spirit at every turn and at every opportunity. In writing to the church at Rome, Paul said: "The good that I want, I do not do, but I practice the very evil that I do not want ... I find ... the principle that evil is present in me, the one who wants to do good. For I joyfully concur with the law of God in the inner man, but I see a different law in the members of my body, waging war against the law of my mind and making me a prisoner of the law of sin which is in my members" (Rom. 7:19, 21-23).

The Old Testament describes King David as a man after God's own heart, but David's story offers testimony that the flesh can rise up suddenly and overtake you. The New Testament has no greater example of spiritual brilliance than Peter. However, Peter can also be seen as the New Testament's greatest example of spiritual failure. The fiery Baptist preacher Vance Havner was once asked how it felt to be a saint of God with temptation under control. He replied, "I pray every day that I don't become the dirty old man I might become at any moment." The great evangelist Billy Sunday said he believed in the devil for two reasons. First, the Bible said so. Second, he had done business with him.

STALEMATE OF THE SOUL

Life for the Christian can also become a deadlock so that we enjoy neither the flesh nor the Spirit, according to Galatians 5:17: "The flesh ... and the Spirit . . are in opposition to one another, so that you may not do the things that you please" — neither in regard to the flesh nor in regard to the Spirit.

When I played football, the coaches would occasionally gather the entire team in a tight circle with a space cleared out in the middle. Then the coaches would call out two names, and those two guys would jump into the middle of the circle and get down in their stances nose-to-nose. Then one of the coaches would blow a whistle and those two guys would slam into each other with such violence that it sounded like thunder, delivering blow-upon-blow until one of them was left standing as the victor. But sometimes there was a stalemate. Their initial strike sounded like pile drivers slamming into each other — their muscles bulged, their feet dug in. They would be growling and snorting, the sweat pouring from their bodies. They were like two huge bulls going head-to-head. Each expended a ton of energy but could not budge the other. Both were left standing. Neither prevailed. There was no victor.

That same thing can happen to us as Christians. Two huge forces collide in our hearts, both strong, both determined, both giving their all—but neither wins. Because of the stalemate we enjoy neither the world of the flesh nor the world of the Spirit. If that is a description of your life, hasn't the time come to see one or the other take the throne of your life? Hasn't the time come to break the deadlock and begin enjoying the things of God? But how?

PRESENT YOURSELF TO GOD

Jesus answered the *how* in John 16:8: the Spirit moves upon the believer's conscience. Paul gives us another suggestion in Romans 6:11-13:

> Consider yourselves to be dead to sin, but alive to God in Christ Jesus. Therefore do not let sin reign in your mortal body that you obey its lusts, and do not go on presenting the members of your body to sin as instruments of unrighteousness; but present yourselves to God as those alive from the dead, and your members as instruments of righteousness to God.

These verses tell us to do three things.

1. Commit.

   Decide the course of your life. Make a bedrock decision right now how you're going to live your life. Are you going to live your life the Self way, or are you going to live your life the Jesus way? Are you going to be a slave to the flesh or a servant to God? Stop straddling the fence. You cannot hold on to both worlds with any measure of success or satisfaction. Be decisive—step up to the plate and swing the bat for the Savior.

2. Don't look back.

   Once you decide for God and the things of God, stop looking back. The things of the world are dead to you. They will only get in the way of enjoying your relationship with God. When Lot fled with his family from Sodom, God said, "Don't look back!" Lot's wife looked back and she turned into a pillar of salt. I'm not telling you that you'll turn into a pillar of salt, but I am telling you that if you keep looking back to the world and longing for it, you will lead a wasted, useless life. Jesus said,

"No one, after putting his hand to the plow and looking back, is fit for the kingdom of God" (Luke 9:62). Stop looking back; keep looking ahead with your eyes firmly focused on the things of God.

3. Present yourself to God.
Each day put yourself under His dominion. Come before God every day and literally release your life into His hands as an instrument for His purpose and usefulness. You may even have to present yourself to God ten times a day. Just do it!

And do it as often as it takes.

The Holy Spirit Workout #5

GETTING INTO FIGHTING SHAPE

Exercise 1

Luke tells us in Acts 2:2 that the Holy Spirit can fill our entire existence, impacting every facet of our life: "and it filled the whole house where they were sitting." How open is your house to the Holy Spirit?

List the major rooms of your life. Then evaluate how open they are to the Holy Spirit. Does the Holy Spirit dwell in the rooms of work, family, play, politics, and other areas of your life?

Exercise 2

Becoming a Christian does not do away with the desires of the flesh. It is normal and natural for the battle between Spirit and flesh to take place within us. The struggle and our determination to win it are signs of our vitality as Christians. Try this exercise in honest self-assessment:

How has the flesh demonstrated its power in your life, in thought and deed?

What are you doing to block the drives of the flesh?

When you were successful, what role did the Holy Spirit play as a battle companion?

When you came to Christ you made the decision to nail the flesh to the cross. You fully intended for the flesh to die on that cross, never again to give you trouble. However, you failed to realize that life would linger in the flesh, that the flesh would call to you and cry out to you and plead with you to release him and set him free.

Chapter Six

Executing
the Flesh

Now the deeds of the flesh are evident ...
– Galatians 5:19

What you will learn in this chapter:
* Three characteristics of a life controlled by the flesh
* The fruit of the Holy Spirit
* What it means to "walk by the Spirit"
* Five steps to make that walk powerful

We learned from Acts 2:2 that, at the point of conversion, God gives to the believer the gift of the Holy Spirit—a gift that comes to us completely, instantaneously, and mightily so that we may serve the Lord with great effectiveness. We also learned from Acts 2:2 that the Holy Spirit comes to us pervasively, invading our hearts with the purpose of taking the leadership role in every area of our existence—no exceptions.

How does the Holy Spirit accomplish this task? First, the Holy Spirit takes the leadership role in the life of the believer by affecting the conscience and contending with our flesh. The

Holy Spirit actively opposes that element within each of us that wants to live without regard for God and the things of God. That is the reason for those colossal clashes within the heart between the forces of darkness and the forces of light. But the Holy Spirit is a Companion Warrior for those who have made a bedrock decision to follow Christ and present themselves to God daily for His purposes and usefulness. Something truly special takes place in the life of those who take the time to be renewed in heart and mind through consistent blocks of time spent with God.

THE CHARACTER-CONDUCT CONNECTION

The Holy Spirit also takes the leadership role in the life of the believer by impacting our character, which in turn, impacts our conduct. To be sure, there are those who treat character and conduct as if they have no connection. However, I believe—and the Bible teaches—that character and conduct are so closely connected that they cannot be separated. Why? Because conduct arises from character. What we do outwardly reflects who we are inwardly. We may sometimes act out of character but not usually. Why? Because our external actions are tied to our internal attitudes.

Prior to life with Christ, inwardly we are flesh. The natural tendency of our lives is to oppose God and His ways. Before coming to Christ, Self is in charge, on the throne, occupying the command-and-control center of our decision-making processes. That is our human makeup. That is who we are. The result is that our fleshly attitudes produce fleshly actions as depicted in Galatians 5:19-21: "The deeds of the flesh are evident, which are: immorality, impurity, sensuality, idolatry, sorcery, enmities, strife, jealousy, outbursts of anger, disputes, dissensions, factions, envying, drunkenness, carousing, and things like these." These actions can be sorted into three major characteristics of the life controlled by the flesh.

A Life of the Flesh: Sexual Misconduct

The life dominated by the flesh is given to sexual misconduct. Immorality, impurity, and sensuality describe those personal impulses that drive us beyond the bounds of God's will to inappropriate premarital relationships, extramarital relationships, and same-sex relationships. The tendency of the flesh on its own — apart from God — is to emphasize the physical so that sex becomes the obsession of life, both in one's thinking and in one's acting.

A Life of the Flesh: Spiritual Misjudgment

Paul uses the words *idolatry* and *sorcery* to say that the life dominated by Self is given not only to sexual misconduct but also to spiritual misjudgment. The flesh attempts to satisfy the emptiness of the heart with things. "More, more, more" is the cry of the inner man. Spiritual misjudgment also means that the flesh is prone to mistake false religion for real religion. A huge array of "isms" permeate our culture because the flesh cannot tell the difference between truth and untruth.

A Life of the Flesh: Social Mismanagement

This form of mismanagement can encompass a large circle of people, a small circle, or even one person. The examples set forth in Galatians 5:20-21 — enmities, strife, jealousy, outbursts of anger, disputes, dissensions, factions, envying — are not meant to be exhaustive, as the last phrase, *and things like these*, indicates. But the list does provide a good illustration of a life ruled by the impulses of the flesh. I doubt seriously that all the items fit any one of us, but all of us can find ourselves somewhere on that list.

A Life of the Holy Spirit

Although Galatians 5:19-21 paints a picture of life controlled by the flesh, the next two verses paint a picture of life controlled by the Holy Spirit. When the Holy Spirit sits on the throne of our lives, the difference is like day and night: The fruit of the Spirit is love, joy, peace, patience, kindness, goodness, faithfulness, gentleness, self-control (Galatians 5:22-23).

- The Holy Spirit produces *love*, that is, the Holy Spirit leads us to live for the success and highest good of others.

- The Holy Spirit produces *joy*. He gives us serenity in the midst of the storm.

- The Holy Spirit produces *peace*. The person living under the impulses of the Spirit will remain calm although the world seems to be crumbling all around.

- The Holy Spirit produces *patience*, enabling us to endure wrong treatment without anger and thoughts of revenge.

- According to Paul, the Holy Spirit produces *kindness*, which enables us to perform positive acts of good on behalf of the one who has committed the wrong.

- When the Holy Spirit has His way in our lives, goodness and faithfulness spring forth from our hearts, giving us aggressive generosity in meeting the needs of others and dependability — the ability to be trusted without fear or apprehension.

- Paul refers to the Spirit-led believer as a person of *gentleness*, one who receives instruction well and applies that instruction to everyday living.

- The Spirit-led person possesses *self-control*; their energies are used for good, not bad. Rather than Self out of-control, this person has Self under control.

The Lingering Flesh

Which picture do you want to depict your life? Will you live your life with Self in charge or the Spirit? If you choose Self over the Spirit, then, according to verse 21, that choice gives evidence that the Holy Spirit does not reside in your heart and you are actually, this moment, living in a state of separation from God. That is, you neither know Him nor belong to Him. However, let's assume that you want your character and conduct to reflect love, joy, peace, patience, kindness, goodness, faithfulness, gentleness, and self-control. How does that happen? Paul, of course, gives us the answer. Galatians 5:16 says, "Walk by the Spirit, and you will not carry out the desire of the flesh."

The presence of the Spirit gives us an alternative to the drives of the flesh. Before Christ came into our hearts, we were at the mercy of those inner longings and cravings. Before Christ came into our hearts, we had no weapon against the demands of the flesh. Now that we've trusted Christ and received the gift of the Holy Spirit, we have the ability not only to fight the flesh but to overpower the flesh.

In this walk by the Spirit, we are to set our eyes on the Spirit, focus on the Spirit, expose ourselves to the Spirit, yield to the Spirit, depend upon the Spirit, sensitize ourselves to the presence of the Spirit every day, and make the leadership of the Spirit the primary factor in our decision-making processes. What we need is not a greater determination, nor a tighter grit of the teeth, nor a firmer set of rules and regulations. What we need is to place ourselves in the embrace of the Spirit every waking moment of the day.

Galations 5:24 says, "Those who belong to Christ Jesus have crucified the flesh with its passions and desires." When we accepted Christ we made a decision to put the flesh to death. Using Paul's terminology, we made a decision to execute the flesh by means of crucifixion. You may ask, "If I decided to execute the flesh, then why am I still struggling with the flesh? Why are the drives of the flesh still alive in my heart?"

Paul's analogy answers that question. Crucifixion was not an instantaneous death. A man nailed to a cross did not die immediately. Death came slowly. Depending on the physical strength and stamina of a man, a criminal could hang on a cross as long as two weeks before death would finally overtake him. For that reason, soldiers had to be placed at the foot of the cross to prevent friends or family from pulling out the nails and setting the criminal free.

Your flesh is that lingering criminal.

When you came to Jesus Christ you made the decision to nail the flesh to the cross. You fully intended for the flesh to die on that cross, never again to give you trouble. However, you failed to realize that life would linger in that flesh. You failed to realize that the flesh would call to you and cry out to you and plead with you to release him and set him free. As a result, you failed to place guards around that crucified flesh. Consequently, Satan can come along and set the flesh free to rule and run your life once again.

DEATH TO THE FLESH

What can you do? Take these five steps in your walk with the spirit.

Step 1: Decide

Decide right now to nail the flesh back to that cross. For many of us, this decision is crucial. Many of us need to decide all over again what we really want. Do you remember the joke about the psychologist? How many psychologists does it take to change a light bulb? Only one, but the light bulb must really want to change. Do you really want to change? The flesh has been your problem all along. The flesh has been giving you nothing but trouble and deserves nothing less than death. Do you truly want to nail the flesh to the cross? Until you make that decision, the flesh will continue to rule your life without restraint or resistance.

Step 2: Refuse to Compromise

You cannot compromise with the flesh. If you try, you'll end up like the woman who wrote a letter to the Internal Revenue Service:

> Dear IRS,
> I can't sleep. Last year when I sent in my income tax, I did not declare all of my income. Enclosed is a check for $325. If I still can't sleep, I'll send you a check for the rest.[1]

Many followers of Jesus Christ are trying to decide how much they can give God and how much they can keep for themselves and still get by. Some are seeking to have a little of the flesh and a little of the Spirit. Compromise is a spiritual killer. Do not be persuaded by the complaints and murmurings of the flesh. The promises of the flesh may bring you pleasure for a season, but ultimately they will bring you great pain — just as they always have. No compromise.

Step 3: Believe in Change

Believe that God can change you. Many people believe that God cannot change them, but such thinking is grossly wrong.

There was a time when experts in track-and-field thought that no man could ever clear seven feet in the high jump or pole vault more than fifteen feet or break four minutes in the mile run. Today those are the goals of high school athletes. God specializes in transforming human character and conduct, even the most pathetic examples imaginable.

But make no mistake: Change often comes about as the result of a long, arduous process. Old habits can be hard to break. The owner of a vast lakefront estate grew tired of his daily commute from the airport to his home. In an effort to save time, he installed pontoons on his plane so he could land on the lake — right in his own backyard. On his next trip, out of habit he began to make his usual approach down the runway at the airport. Just before touching down he realized that he couldn't land on the runway — he had no wheels! He barely averted disaster as he quickly pulled the nose of the plane toward the sky. He continued on to the lake, landing the plane without incident. As he sat in the cockpit, visibly shaken, he said to himself, *I don't know what got into me. That's the dumbest thing I've ever done!* Then, he opened the door, stepped out of the plane — and into the lake.

Lifelong habits can be hard to change, but through time your life will be greatly altered. Don't give up. Don't quit after one failure. Don't quit after many failures. Keep getting up. Keep coming back to God. Keep moving forward. God will change you magnificently.

Step 4: Stay on Guard

Place guards around the criminal you have nailed to the cross. Spend time with God each day through Bible reading and prayer. Never fail to post that guard. Give yourself to corporate worship regularly. Never fail to post that guard. Spend time with friends who are strong in their faith. Never fail to post that guard. Have at least one trusted person who can call you into accountability. Without the appropriate guards standing at the foot of the cross, Satan will take down the fleshly nature and give it renewed life.

Step 5: Listen

Be alert for the inner movement and impressions of the Holy Spirit. The more you listen and obey those impressions, the more you will sense the leadership and voice of the Spirit within. "Walk by the Spirit, and you will not carry out the desires of the flesh."

NOTES

[1] Marion Aldridge, "Sermon Illustrations: Character," *Proclaim: The Pastor's Journal for Biblical Preaching* (October-December 1990): 28.

Holy Spirit Workout #6

HOW TO CONQUER THE FLESH

Exercise 1
Galatians 5:19-21 lists these characteristics of a life controlled by the flesh: immorality, impurity, sensuality, idolatry, sorcery, enmities, strife, jealousy, outbursts of anger, disputes, dissentions, factions, envying, drunkenness, carousing and things like these.

Do any of these traits present a danger to your walk with the Spirit? Which of these fleshly actions do you most need the Holy Spirit's help with?

Exercise 2
Galatians 5:22-23 lists the fruit of a life controlled by the Spirit: love, joy, peace, patience, kindness, goodness, faithfulness, gentleness, self-control.

How evident is this fruit in your daily life? Under what conditions do you usually fail to display the Spirit's fruit?

Exercise 3
Although when you came to Jesus Christ you made a decision to nail the flesh to the cross, you also know that the flesh still lives and can sometimes regain control of us.

What guards can you surround yourself with so that you keep the flesh nailed upon the cross? Who or what is in your regiment of Guards Against the Flesh: Prayer? Worship? Bible study? Friends? What are the most effective guards for you?

Multitudes of Christians have been dancing for a long time, but without the music. They have been living by the written score, but they have never heard the symphony.

Chapter Seven

Explaining *the* Unexplainable

How shall you believe if I tell you of heavenly things?
– John 3:12

What you will learn in this chapter:

* Why the Holy Spirit is like the wind
* How God can add years to your life
* The symphony that changed a man's life
* How to see the unseen

There is one more characteristic revealed about the Holy Spirit in Acts 2:2: "Suddenly there came from heaven a noise like a violent rushing wind." Notice the word translated *wind*. On the day of Pentecost — as God began the unprecedented era in which He would pour out His Spirit upon all who would follow Jesus Christ — those gathered in the upper room heard a noise that sounded like the blowing of a forceful, powerful wind. Why does Luke depict the Holy Spirit as the sound of moving air?

THE HOLY WIND

The word for *spirit* in the original languages of both the Old and New Testaments is often translated *wind*. The Holy Spirit and the Holy Wind could be synonyms. Certainly the Holy Spirit is not wind, but the Bible does teach that the Holy Spirit is like the wind.

Think about it. You can feel the rush of wind across your body. You can witness the movement of wind as it blows through the trees. You can give testimony to the presence of wind as a leaf, or piece of paper, or some other item being pushed across the lawn or down the street. You can point to overwhelming evidence that the wind is all around you, but you cannot actually see the wind. You cannot hold the wind in your hand, nor can you capture the wind and place it in a container for safekeeping. You can take advantage of the wind if you know how, but you cannot say: "I see the wind. This is where the wind begins and this is where it ends."

The same is true for the Holy Spirit. There are times when you can actually sense the Holy Spirit's presence flowing through your body. There are times when you can witness the movement of the Spirit as He impacts the circumstances that come against your life. You can give testimony to the activity of the Spirit as He influences those for whom you have been praying. You can point to overwhelming evidence that the Holy Spirit is all around you, but you cannot actually see the Holy Spirit. You cannot physically hold the Holy Spirit in your hand, nor can you capture the Holy Spirit and place Him in a container for safekeeping. You can take advantage of the Spirit's presence and power if you know how, but you cannot say: "I see the Holy Spirit. This is where the Spirit begins and this is where it ends."

THE HOLY PROOF

If I tell you there is a bone in my leg, you could say, "Oh yeah?

Prove it!" And if I really wanted to, I could take an X-ray of my leg and show you an image of that bone. If you didn't believe the X-ray, I could slice my leg open, pull back the flesh, and say: "See, there it is. I told you there is a bone in my leg!" If I tell you that the Holy Spirit inhabits my life, that the presence of God actually and literally resides in my body, you could say, "Prove it!" And, truth is, I couldn't — at least not in the way I proved there was a bone in my leg. I could point to abounding evidence of the Spirit's reality, but it would not include an X-ray image or a surgical procedure. The reality of the Holy Spirit is discerned like the reality of the wind—you cannot actually see the wind but you can observe unmistakable evidence of its existence.

So, when the Holy Spirit comes upon our lives, He comes suddenly, powerfully, and inexplicably. When the Holy Spirit takes up residence in our hearts, there is much about His residency that simply cannot be explained in rational terms. Scientific research, mathematical computations, and humanistic-secular reasoning are useless in explaining the Holy Spirit's habitation of our lives.

HOW GOD ADDS YEARS TO YOUR LIFE

In the article "Eight Ways To Look—and Feel—Years Younger," the author's last suggestion is "Consider your soul":

> Growing evidence links a belief in God to better physical health. In 22 studies, frequent churchgoers had lower rates of many illnesses, from hypertension and heart disease to tuberculosis and cervical cancer. Scientists aren't sure why. Jeffrey S. Levin at Eastern Virginia Medical School in Norfolk, Virginia, notes: "It might be that being more religious fosters a healthier lifestyle, offers greater social support or provides a buffer against stress. Or it could be that hope

and optimism somehow bolster the immune system." For example, when doctors examined men over 65 who had been admitted to a veterans hospital in Durham, North Carolina, they found those patients who said religion was very important to them were less likely to become depressed—a feeling that by itself can hinder recovery.

Dr. Randolf C. Byrd, a cardiologist, created a stir in medical circles when he had volunteers pray daily for one group of patients in the coronary care unit at San Francisco General Medical Center. A second group of heart disease patients served as a control group. Although neither the patients nor the doctors knew who got the prayers, those in the prayed-for group were five times less likely to require antibiotics and were less apt to need ventilators to help them breathe.

Levin concludes: "The evidence strongly suggests faith in God truly is linked to a long, healthy life."[1]

Let's analyze this article excerpt from a spiritual perspective. The author of "Eight Ways to Look—and Feel—Years Younger" presents evidence to readers in support of the point that spiritual health can significantly affect physical health. But where does that proof come from? Scientific studies which produce data that can be analyzed, charted, plotted, and held out as tangible proof that the intangible exists. The spiritual has, once again, been reduced to the empirical.

The article's reliance on empiricism merely reflects what is pervasive in our culture: the inability to live with realities that defy explanation. If you are one of those who want everything packaged in a neat, mathematical box with a scientific ribbon on top, then you are going to miss the most exciting realities that life has to offer. Man is far more than the combination of designated chemical elements, far more than a mass of interrelated physical properties. Man is not only physical, he is spiritual. In fact, man may rightly be said to be more spiritual than physical because the physical is slowly dying and will one day perish. Only the spiritual is capable of living forever. Evidence of this truth permeates the environment in which we live. It is everywhere and yet nowhere—like the wind.

A spiritual teacher can elucidate major and minor theological hypotheses about the Holy Spirit or even dig out the Greek roots and serve them on a platter. But if you insist on guiding your life only by what you can hold in your hands and by what you can see with your eyes, then you will never know the truest pleasures of an in-depth relationship with God. The Holy Spirit is the spice of the Christian's life, and ultimately the Holy Spirit defies human explanation.

A MIGHTY DULL DANCE

Max Lucado has suggested that the Holy Spirit is to Christianity what music is to dancing. In an article appearing in *Discipleship Journal* he wrote:

> We Christians are prone to follow the book while ignoring the music. We master the doctrine, outline the chapters, memorize the dispensations, debate the rules, and stiffly step down the dance floor of life with no music in our hearts. We measure each step, calibrate each turn, and flop into bed each night exhausted from another day of dancing by the book.
>
> Dancing with no music is tough stuff.
>
> Jesus knew that. For that reason, on the night before His death He introduced the disciples to the

song maker of the Trinity, the Holy Spirit. When I go away, I will send the Helper (the Holy Spirit) to you.[2]

Is Lucado denigrating the Bible? Absolutely not! Rather, he is calling for a balance. Jesus said in John 4:24, "God is spirit, and those who worship Him must worship Him in spirit and truth." I believe Jesus means that the algorithms of the physical are necessary, but the essence of life is not in the algorithms. The tangible must be included, but the intangible must not be excluded. In holding to what can be explained, we need to also make room for what cannot be explained.

Some may ask, "Are you telling me that I can throw explanation out the window and live by experience alone?" No. I am telling you to know the Scripture, but I am also telling you to know the Spirit. As Max Lucado might say, the Scripture without the Spirit makes a mighty dull dance.

NICODEMUS AND THE SIMPLICITY OF BELIEF

The problem we face is not merely that of the modern mind. Even centuries ago there were those who missed God because they mistook logic for life. In the third chapter of John's gospel, for example, we are introduced to a man who had been dancing for a long time without the music. This man had the score but had never heard the symphony. Then he met Jesus:

> Now there was a man of the Pharisees, named Nicodemus, a ruler of the Jews; this man came to Jesus by night, and said to Him, "Rabbi, we know that You have come from God as a teacher; for no one can do these signs unless God is with Him."
>
> Jesus answered and said to him, "Truly, truly, I say to you, unless one is born again he cannot see the kingdom of God." Nicodemus said to him, "How can

a man be born when he is old? He cannot enter a second time into his mother's womb and be born, can he?" Jesus answered, "Truly, truly, I say to you, unless one is born of water and the Spirit he cannot enter into the kingdom of God. That which is born of the flesh is flesh, and that which is born of the Spirit is spirit. Do not be amazed that I said to you, 'You must be born again.' The wind blows were it wishes and you hear the sound of it, but do not know where it comes from and where it is going; so is everyone who is born of the Spirit." Nicodemus said to Him, "How can these things be?" (John 3:1-9)

The story of Nicodemus conveys three principles about dancing to the Spirit's symphony.

Principle 1: You Can't Grasp the Spiritual by Means of the Physical

You would think that religious people, especially, would know that. Yet, in the above story as told by John, we discover a highly religious man who had been trying to reach God by purely physical strategies. Nicodemus was a Pharisee, a man who had committed his life to the keeping of every detail of God's law. Before becoming a Pharisee, Nicodemus, like other candidates, had to stand before three witnesses and pledge that he would meticulously observe and follow every point of the scribal law, which was a compilation of thousands of rules and regulations that had been derived from God's law. For instance, the fourth commandment says, "Remember the Sabbath day, to keep it holy. Six days you shall labor and do all your work, but the seventh day is a Sabbath of the Lord your God; in it you shall not do any work" (Ex. 20:8-10). Through the centuries, the Jewish scribes had developed thousands of trivial guidelines about the Sabbath, and those guidelines spelled out what could and couldn't be done on the seventh day. A Pharisee vowed to study and keep all the rules and regulations, down to the last jot and tittle.

Nicodemus had pledged to live his life by the book, to know God by doing and not doing certain things. That seemed to be all right — until Jesus came along. When Nicodemus encountered Jesus he began to hear something he had never heard before and to experience something he had never experienced before. For the first time in his life, Nicodemus came face-to-face with the melody of heaven. For the first time in his life, Nicodemus was overwhelmed by the symphony of the Holy Spirit. For the first time in his life he caught a glimpse of the kingdom of God and wanted to enter that kingdom. But how?

Principle 2: Only the Spiritual Can Grasp the Spiritual

Jesus said, "Nicodemus, you must be born again." Nicodemus responded, "How can a man be born when he is old? Can he enter a second time into his mother's womb?" This is a communication problem: Jesus is talking about spiritual things; Nicodemus is thinking about physical things. Jesus is talking about life; Nicodemas is thinking about logic. Jesus is talking about relationship; Nicodemus is thinking about ritual. Jesus is talking about the Spirit of God bursting upon a person's life; Nicodemus is thinking about pledges and vows made under a system of stringent rules and detailed regulations. Jesus is offering something that is beyond explanation; Nicodemus is asking for something that can be explained.

In other words, Jesus is saying: Nicodemus, you've got to break out of your earth-bound way of thinking and make room in your life for an invasion of God's presence. Nicodemus, you have been enslaved and limited by the bonds of human reasoning; you must be emancipated and set free by the inexplicable movement and power of the Holy Spirit upon your life. Nicodemus, the flesh understands nothing but the flesh, the physical knows nothing but the physical. Accept the reality of the Spirit and you will see the kingdom of God. Open your heart and mind to the reality of the Spirit and right now your eyes will be opened to an amazing new world that anxiously awaits your active participation.

Principle 3: The Spiritual Defies Human Calculation
Nicodemus exclaimed in verse 9, "How can these things be?" Jesus responded in verse 12: "If I told you earthly things and you do not believe, how shall you believe if I tell you heavenly things?"

Jesus is saying: Nicodemus, I've made this as simple as anyone can possibly make it. Looking at the wind is as close as you will come to an explanation that can be grasped by the finite mind. The wind blows where it wishes and you hear the sound of it, but do not know where it comes from and where it is going; so is everyone who is born of the Spirit.

A fellow seminary student once said of John 3:8: "We rationalize, psychologize, and demythologize until we reach the same place as the journalist who wrote, 'We know now that there is no such thing as the supernatural.' Jesus is saying, 'Nicodemas, stop explaining and arguing. Believe.'"

THE REALITY OF THE UNSEEN
Unfortunately, there are many who refuse to believe unless somehow they can see the realities of which we speak. However, faith in the unseen has been — and will always be — an essential element to knowing God and the workings of God. Many in the first century who encountered firsthand the miraculous power of Jesus Christ refused to accept the validity of what they saw with their own eyes. Even then, hard facts

were not enough — in and of themselves — to convince some-one of the authenticity of the spiritual dimension.

Jesus told a poignant story in Luke 16 about a rich man who cried out from Hades, asking Abraham to send Lazarus to his five brothers for the purpose of warning them about the place of torment that had unexpectedly engulfed his life. Abraham re-sponded, "If they do not listen to Moses and the Prophets, they will not be persuaded even if someone rises from the dead."

There was no hope for the tormented man or his brothers. Those who reject the witness of Scripture will also reject indis-putable facts that offer proof of the nonphysical world. The wind provides all the proof they needed or you will ever need. Put away your calculator. Close your science book. Shut down your computer network—and simply believe.

Then, and only then, will you hear the music of the Holy Spirit.

NOTES

[1] Sue Browder, "Eight Ways to Look—and Feel—Years Younger," *Reader's Digest*, September 1995, 151.

[2] Max Lucado, "Music for the Dance," *Discipleship Journal* 91 (January/February 1996): 40.

The Holy Spirit Workout #7

TRAINING TO SEE THE UNSEEN

Exercise 1
Besides the wind and the Holy Spirit, name three other phenomena you accept the reality of without being able to see them. What enables you to accept them?

Exercise 2
As important as it is to know Scripture, what other elements are essential to you for a joyful, celebrative Christian life? List and explain each.

Exercise 3
This chapter compares Christianity without the Spirit to a dance without music. Create some of your own comparisons that illustrate how empty Christianity can be without the Holy Spirit. Example: A child's room without a child.

THE POWER FOR *L*IVING LIBRARY

PART THREE

What They Saw

The Holy Spirit does for us today what the fire and smoke did for Israel some 3,400 years ago.

Chapter Eight

ℋalos of ℱire

And there appeared to them tongues as of fire distributing themselves, and they rested on each one of them.
– Acts 2:3

What you will learn in this chapter:

* Why the Holy Spirit cannot be domesticated
* The difference between the "hows" and "whats" of God's miracles
* Why the Holy Spirit has been placed in your life
* Four ways the Holy Spirit leads us today

The second chapter of Acts records for us the event that ushered in a riveting new age for those who followed the God of Israel. No longer would the presence and power of God be given only to a few believers, but to all who choose to stake their lives upon Jesus Christ. Race would not be a barrier; gender would not be a barrier; poverty would not be a barrier; slavery would not be a barrier. What we find in the first four verses of Acts 2 is the inaugural ceremony of the Holy Spirit's outpouring as witnessed by 120 first-century disciples. Each element in the first four verses is like a coronation trumpet announcing the fulfillment of those incredible prophecies made by Joel 800 years before:

> And it shall be in the last days," God says, "that I will pour forth of my Spirit on all mankind; and your sons and your daughters shall prophesy, and your young men shall see visions, and your old men shall dream dreams; even on My bondslaves, both men and women, I will in those days pour forth of my Spirit" (Joel 2:28-29).

In Acts 2, the last days had finally dawned.

LIKE A FIRE BLAZING WITHIN

The Holy Spirit is God's precious gift to every believer. Amazing, isn't it? Even more amazing is the sad reality that so many Christians are leading what have been called "lives of quiet mediocrity."[1] They are either ignorant of the Holy Spirit's presence, or they are afraid of what the Holy Spirit wants to do. Almost thirty years ago an Anglican pastor wrote a book out of his concern that many within the circles of Christendom had domesticated the Holy Spirit:

> The Holy Spirit is a disturbing influence. Let him therefore be paid lip service, but for all practical purposes be shut up in the Bible where he can do no harm.... it would be very embarrassing and doctrinally untidy if the Holy Spirit were to speak to men today.
>
> Many [within the church] ... have heard in a vague way about the Holy Spirit, but have either put it all down to typical ecclesiastical in-talk, or assumed that it was not intended for ordinary folks like themselves.

> For all practical purposes, the Holy Spirit [has been]
> discounted [by millions of Christians]. [To them]
> Christianity is a matter of churchgoing, of soldering
> on and trying to do one's best ....,[2]

Please don't miss what I want to tell you here: The second chapter of Acts is shockingly clear that the Holy Spirit cannot be domesticated. The Holy Spirit is like a red-hot fire blazing within the deepest recesses of our hearts. In fact, take away the Holy Spirit and the act of following Jesus Christ is like watching a black-and-white, silent movie out of the 1920s. But when the flames of the Holy Spirit are fanned within our hearts, following Jesus Christ is comparable to watching state-of-the-art cinematography with surround sound and brilliant colors.

This fiery Holy Spirit is exactly what Acts 2:3 describes: "And there appeared to them [that is, to the 120 men and women gathered in a second-story room of a house located somewhere in Jerusalem] tongues as of fire distributing themselves, and they rested on each one of them." Can you imagine? The men and women in this room saw themselves enveloped by what looked like tongue-shaped flames (what they really were, in actuality, remains a mystery), but these fiery tongues appeared to break apart and group themselves in such a way that each person present seemed to wear a glowing halo of fire.

Wouldn't you like to have been there? I would. And wouldn't you love to get some answers to physiological questions about what happened in that room? Some people come to a verse like this and they suddenly feel like that little boy who arrived home from Sunday school and was asked by his mother what his teacher had taught him that day. The boy replied, "Well Mom, the teacher told us about Moses leading the children of Israel across the Red Sea." Then the mom asked her small son to tell her the story. "Well, Mom, the people of Israel were standing by the Red Sea and the Egyptian army came rushing at them. Moses then ordered a huge company of tanks to form a wall that would keep the Egyptians back. Then he called in the Israeli Air Force to take out their long-range weapons. Meanwhile, the Army Corp of Engineers built a bridge across the Red Sea, and when the last Israeli crossed over and the Egyptian army was in the middle of it, the engineers blew the whole thing to pieces."

The mom asked, "Son, is that really what your teacher told you about Moses and the Red Sea?" To which the boy replied, "No, but if I told you what she really said, you wouldn't believe it in a million years."

There are times when I want to ask, how did God do that? That happens when I read Acts 2:3. How did God do that? How can this phenomenon be explained? Yet the Bible almost never explains the *hows*. The problem many of us face is getting so hung-up on the hows that we miss the whats. If I could place in your hand a scientific treatise written by Albert Einstein that unveiled the hows of verse 3, you would be missing the point entirely if that is all you understood. In the final analysis, the hows don't really matter, only the whats do. Here's the question for us today:

What does verse 3 mean, and what difference does it make in our lives?

THE INTERPRETATION

Here are the important questions: What does verse 3 mean? What does verse 3 tell us about the operation of the Holy Spirit in the lives of Christ's disciples? What startling, life-changing revelation comes to us out of these tongues of flame and halos of fire?

To answer those questions, turn to Exodus 13. Remember, the only Bible available to the men and women of Acts 2 was the

Old Testament. The gospel stories of Matthew, Mark, Luke, and John had not been written. In fact, two decades would pass before any book of the New Testament would come forth. Thus, the way these first-century followers interpreted this experience depended upon their understanding of certain Old Testament passages. One of those passages is Exodus 13:21-22:

> The Lord was going before them in a pillar of cloud by day to lead them on the way, and in a pillar of fire by night to give them light, that they might travel by day and by night. He did not take away the pillar of cloud by day, nor the pillar of fire by night, from before the people.

The setting of Exodus 13 is the deliverance of Israel from a four hundred year bondage in Egypt. Israel had been set free from slavery to the world system, so to speak, for the express purpose of worshiping Jehovah-God and serving as His light to the nations. The closing verses of Exodus 13 reveal at least four characteristics about God's relationship to His newly released children.

God Provided Specific Leadership

These verses tell us that God did not gain Israel's deliverance and then leave them to their own choices and devices. Verse 21 says, "He was going before them," which means God stayed out front while they came behind. Israel went where God went rather than where they might have wanted to go. Why? God had created a specific plan for their lives; He had engineered a specific course of action. God did not say: Now that you're free, what would you like to do? Absolutely not! God said: I'm going to lead. You follow! That is the rifle shot of the entire Exodus experience. God provided specific leadership.

God Provided Obvious Leadership

He used a billowing column of smoke to lead them by day and a blazing column of fire to lead them by night. God removed all the guesswork. There could be no mistaking God's direction for their journey. No one could say, "Lord, I didn't realize. Lord, how could I have known?"

God Provided All-Encompassing Leadership

His leadership was for all occasions. He went before Israel by day and by night. No matter the event, regardless of the circumstance, God set forth His direction and desire. Not only did He lead them by night when things could be more frightening and confusing, but He also led them by day when things were less complicated. God did not say: You figure out the easy stuff; only come to Me when things get tough. If it concerned Israel, it concerned God. If it had to do with Israel, it had to do with God.

God Provided Constant Leadership

Verse 22 says, "He did not take away the pillar of cloud by day, nor the pillar of fire by night." Israel never had to worry that they would wake up one morning and God would be gone. God's leadership did not depend upon their perfection but upon His faithfulness. God never failed to provide leadership.

THE APPLICATION

So what does God's leadership for Israel have to do with Acts 2:3? That was then, this is now. Quite simply, the tongues of fire in the third verse of Acts 2 tell us that the Holy Spirit — who is God Himself, literally and actually present in our lives — does for us today exactly what the smoke and fire did for Israel some 3,400 years ago:

- The Holy Spirit is the fire of God's presence within our hearts.
- The Holy Spirit is the smoke of God's guidance over-shadowing our minds.
- The Holy Spirit is God going before us.
- The Holy Spirit is God shining His light into our lives.
- The Holy Spirit is God personally interacting with those who have staked their lives on Jesus Christ.

Acts 2:3 tells us that the primary role of the Holy Spirit is that of leadership. But the Spirit's leadership is not merely for the pastor or the church staff or some poor missionary in a desolate, faraway land. Take note that these tongues of fire did not just rest on Peter and the other ten who made up the inner circle of Christ's disciples at that moment. No, the tongues of fire rested upon them all.

The rifle shot of Acts 2:3 is this: The Holy Spirit has taken up residence in your life for the purpose of leading you. For the follower of Jesus Christ, the Holy Spirit is the commander, the pilot, the captain, the helmsman, the chief executive officer. The Holy Spirit serves as the judge of every thought, the head-master of every attitude, and the director of every action. If you are a Christian, the Holy Spirit has been placed in your life for the express purpose of leading you.

Before God saved you, He first created a marvelous plan for your life, and He wants you to know that plan. God saved you because He wants to lead you, and He wants to lead you in obvious ways. He doesn't want you to guess about life's choices and decisions. He will lead you in every instance. Every care can be confidently cast upon Him.

Follow the leadership of the Holy Spirit and the chaos becomes order—at least the inner person can know order in the midst of chaotic circumstances. Follow the leadership of the

Holy Spirit and the confusion becomes peace—at least the inner person can know peace in the midst of a volatile environment.

How do you follow the leadership of the Spirit? How do you wear that halo of fire? We'll talk about that in the next chapter.

NOTES

[1] Timothy Riter, "Living Supernaturally," *Discipleship Journal* 91 (January/February 1996): 52.

[2] Michael Green, *I Believe in the Holy Spirit* (Grand Rapids: William B. Eerdmans Publishing Company, 1975), p. 12.

The Holy Spirit Workout #8

FINDING THE FIRE WITHIN

Do you agree that many Christians lead "lives of quiet mediocrity" when it comes to the Holy Spirit? That they have tried to domesticate the Holy Spirit? To help understand the difference between a life led by the fire and smoke of the Holy Spirit and a life that is not, complete the comparison chart.

My prayer life is—

- *When the Holy Spirit is aflame:* Daily, direct and personal, a source of guidance and strength that flows from my passionate connection to God.
- *When the Holy Spirit is cold:* Ritualistic, usually led by others. I think of other things while mouthing the most important words in life.

My Bible study life is —
When the Holy Spirit is aflame / When the Holy Spirit is cold

My decision-making efforts are —
When the Holy Spirit is aflame / When the Holy Spirit is cold

My witnessing life is —
When the Holy Spirit is aflame / When the Holy Spirit is cold

My job is —
When the Holy Spirit is aflame / When the Holy Spirit is cold

My devotion to my family is—
When the Holy Spirit is aflame / When the Holy Spirit is cold

The Holy Spirit leads us, and He does so — first and foremost — by bringing into personal view the universe of insights that reside in the Bible.

Chapter Nine

The Spirit and the Word

All who are being led by the Spirit of God,
these are the sons of God.
– Romans 8:14

What you will learn in this chapter:

* How the Holy Spirit leads the believer
* Why Christians are not dumb and boring
* Where to put your spiritual lamp
* Brittany's lesson

"All who are being led by the Spirit of God, these are the sons of God." Those words form the heart of Paul's letter to the church at Rome. In his declaration, we discover one of the pieces of unmistakable evidence that a man or woman has come to new life in Jesus Christ. What is that evidence? The leadership of the Holy Spirit. There is a vital connection between *sonship* and *leadership.* The person who is truly linked to God through the life of His Son is also linked to God through the leadership of His Spirit.

When a person comes to Christian faith, that person stakes

their life on what God did for them in the past by means of Jesus Christ. But there's more. When a person comes to Christian faith, that person also stakes their life on what God wants to do for them in the present by means of the Holy Spirit.

Jesus did something for us in the past. The Holy Spirit does something for us now. One of the proofs that we honestly believe in what Jesus did for us back then is the way we follow the leadership of the Holy Spirit today.

We have already learned that the Holy Spirit provides specific, obvious, all-encompassing and constant leadership. The question before us in this chapter is: How does the Holy Spirit provide leadership for the believer?

THE LEADERSHIP OF UNDERSTANDING AND APPLICATION

The first way the Holy Spirit leads is by helping us to understand the Bible. The Holy Spirit helps us comprehend the biblical axioms of divine wisdom, and then He assists us in applying those axioms to our lives. He shows us how God's truth intersects with the choices and decisions that confront us. The Holy Spirit is the bridge that spans the chasm between the ancient world and the modern world, enabling us to use biblical principles to answer life's questions of meaning and purpose.

If you have ever understood anything of significance from the Bible, that understanding resulted from the leadership of the Holy Spirit. If you have ever read a passage of Scripture and your life has been challenged, that challenge resulted from the leadership of the Holy Spirit. If you have ever heard a sermon and your heart has been convicted, that conviction resulted from the leadership of the Holy Spirit. If you have ever participated in a Bible study and the inner person was driven to change, that change resulted from the leadership of the Holy Spirit.

WHAT ABOUT NON-CHRISTIANS?

Look at 1 Corinthians 2:14: "A natural man does not accept the things of the Spirit of God, for they are foolishness to him; and he cannot understand them, because they are spiritually appraised."

Paul is telling us that a non-Christian—that is, a person who has never staked his or her life on Jesus Christ, therefore a person in whom the Holy Spirit does not reside—cannot possibly understand scriptural truth. To the non-Christian, listening to biblical precepts and principles is like a Chinese kindergarten class listening to an English-speaking economist give an address on the advantages of the free-market system. There is simply no connection.

Paul tells us in verse 14 that even if a non-Christian could understand scriptural truth, he or she would not accept that truth. That is, a non-Christian would not hold to biblical guidance as an acceptable philosophy of life. A non-Christian may say, "I see what you're saying, but I don't care. I operate my life by an altogether different point of view."

Paul tells us in verse 14 that scriptural truth is not only seen by the non-Christian as incomprehensible and unacceptable, scriptural truth is actually regarded as foolishness. The Greek word Paul uses for *foolishness* is the basis of our English word *moron*. To the non-Christian, the statutes and commandments of God's Word are utter nonsense.

IGNORANT, BORING CHRISTIANS

Have you ever wondered why the film producers in Hollywood love to make Christians look stupid? Here's the answer. They think we are stupid! Have you ever wondered why the leaders of the mainstream media love to make Christians look boring and ignorant? Paul gave us the answer nineteen centuries ago. They think we are boring and ignorant! What's more, the entertainment and news industries will remain that way until strong, daring men and women of God begin filtering into those businesses. Why? Without the leadership of the Holy Spirit, no one can possibly gain access to the enlightenment that is found in the Bible. Without the leadership of the Holy Spirit, a person is blind to the sphere of reality rooted in the Bible.

The irony of it all is that the non-Christian who thinks he's hot is really not. The non-Christian who believes himself or herself to have it together is the one who is actually ignorant and foolish. Why? First Corinthians 2:6 gives us two reasons: "We ... speak wisdom among those who are mature; a wisdom, however, not of this age nor of the rulers of this age, who are passing away." Those without Christ are ignorant because they depend upon a system of thinking that is rooted in *this age*, that is, in the tides of popular philosophy. As a result, they guide their lives by whatever theories or ideologies are fashionable at the moment.

Paul also tells us that those without Christ are ignorant because they rely upon a system of thinking that is designed by *the rulers of this age*. The choices and decisions of non-Christians are heavily influenced by the darlings of society – those at the top of the music charts, on the best-seller lists, starring in the latest movies, or seen on TV as the current political pundit and latest educational guru.

Those who follow the darlings of society truly believe themselves to be free thinkers, but 1 Corinthians 2:6 says they are nothing more than unwitting slaves locked within the narrow confines of their culture—a culture that will ultimately go down as a momentary blip on the radar screen of history. The disciples of society's darlings are little more than parrots mimicking their peers.

THE THOUGHTS OF GOD

The true free thinkers are those who have a personal relationship with Jesus Christ. Because of that relationship, they are empowered by the Holy Spirit to think the thoughts of God after Him. Rather than following a system of thinking that is built upon the sands of momentary fads, they stand confidently upon the rock-solid wisdom of the ages—a wisdom by which God created the heavens and earth, a wisdom by which God judges the actions and motives of man, a wisdom that perpetually governs the flow of the universe. This wisdom, of course, is found in the pages of the Bible and, by means of the Holy Spirit, is freely given to those who choose Jesus Christ as Savior and Lord.

IS YOUR LAMP UNDER A BASKET?

The Holy Spirit leads us first and foremost by illuminating the universe of insights that reside in the Bible. What does that mean in practical terms? Look at the fourth chapter of Mark's gospel, verses 21, and 24-25:

> A lamp is not brought to be put under a basket, is it, or under a bed? Is it not brought to be put on the lampstand? Take care what you listen to. By your standard of measure it will be measured to you; and more will be given you besides. For whoever has, to him more shall be given; and whoever does not have, even what he has shall be taken away from him.

What is the purpose of a lamp? Is its purpose to be placed under a basket so that its light is hidden? Is its purpose to be stored under a bed so that its light is concealed? No. A lamp is to be positioned in such a way that an entire room or area is exposed to its light.

If I want the Holy Spirit to lead me, then I must be exposed to the Bible. The Holy Spirit does not work in a vacuum. He operates within the framework of biblical light. If I throw my Bible on a shelf and leave it there all week, that is about as smart as taking the light off the kitchen ceiling and putting it under a bucket on the kitchen table. If I shove my Bible in a drawer and let it baby-sit my socks all week, that is about as intelligent as removing the light from my walk-in closet and stuffing it under my bed. Without exposure to the Word of God, the Holy Spirit is strangely silent when a person faces important decisions and choices.

TAKE CARE WHAT YOU LISTEN TO

Notice the beginning of Mark 4:24: "Take care what you listen to." What are you listening to? If the Holy Spirit is going to lead you, then choosing the Word of God as your chief source of philosophy is imperative. There are many voices clamoring for our attention. There are a multitude of "isms," schemes, and theories out there. However, God will not be one voice among many. He does not do business with those who consider His will as a possible alternative. If you want the Holy Spirit to give you precision leadership, then solitary devotion to the teachings of the Bible is requisite. When it comes to standards of right and wrong, which voice is it going to be? When it comes to the principles by which you conduct your social life and your business life and your home life, which voice will it be?

My daughter Brittany used to come by my office every day after school, and she hung around until I was ready to go home. On the way home we commonly discussed various school issues and life issues. Regardless of the issue, I inevitably asked her this question: "What is the basis of your decision-making process?" If you're interested at all in the leadership of the Holy Spirit, then the basis of your decision-making process will be the Word of God. The Holy Spirit draws water only from the well of the Word. The Holy Spirit will never lead you contrary to the Word of God.

MORE BEGETS MORE

Look at the end of Mark 4:24 and all of verse 25: "By your standard of measure it will be measured to you and more will be given you besides. For whoever has, to him more shall be given; and whoever does not have, even what he has shall be taken away from him."

Mark is warning me that if I neglect or ignore the Word of God, then the chances increase that what little insight I possess will be taken away.

Fortunately, Mark also says the converse is true: The leadership of the Holy Spirit in my life is commensurate to the time I spend allowing the Bible to engage my heart and mind. The more I read the Bible, the more I can expect the Holy Spirit to provide leadership. The more I meditate on the Bible, the more I can expect the Holy Spirit to increase my sensitivity regarding the things of God. The more I listen to sound biblical teachers, the more I can expect the Holy Spirit to open my spiritual eyes and ears to the deep realities of God.

If I will spread my life before the Word of God on a regular basis, then the Holy Spirit will give me the ability to think the thoughts of God.

The Holy Spirit Workout #9

LETTING YOURSELF BE LED

"Seek and ye shall find." Truer words have never been spoken when it comes to the leadership of the Holy Spirit. He dwells within us, prepared to give guidance and to reveal the principles and truths we need to stay on God's path. But we cannot be passive recipients of leadership. We must actively seek the Holy Spirit's guidance through Bible reading and study, through prayer and meditation. These are the lights that the Holy Spirit uses to illuminate our decisions and actions. How bright are your lights?

Exercise

Step 1: Describe a life-issue that you are currently facing.

Step 2: List ways to increase your chances of seeing God's viewpoint: Bible study, prayer, discussions with a spiritual leader in your church.

Step 3: Explore each of those options.

Step 4: Describe what you believe the Holy Spirit is guiding you to do.

We can no longer assume that everyone who walks through the doors of a church knows the difference between right and wrong.

Chapter Ten

Distinguishing Right and Wrong

When He, the Spirit of truth, comes, He will guide you into all the truth.
— John 16:13

In this chapter, you will learn:

* A Christian's definition of truth
* The origin of truth
* Three ways the Holy Spirit speaks to us
* Five characteristics of statutes and commandments
* Why the homes of some Christian families are in chaos

"When He, the Spirit of truth, comes, He will guide you into all the truth." Those words reassure us there is a vital link between the presence of the Holy Spirit and personal guidance. That is, when the Holy Spirit takes up residence in our lives His primary purpose is to provide individual leadership. The Holy Spirit becomes to us an advisor, a counselor, and a teacher. The Holy Spirit gives us direction. The Holy Spirit instructs us in the decision-making process.

Those words of John also tell us that there is a vital link between the guidance of the Holy Spirit and the illumination of truth. That is, when the Holy Spirit takes up residence in our lives His primary purpose is to provide individual leadership by bringing us face-to-face with the truth for the purpose of guiding us in the decision-making process. Those two insights lead us to ask two questions. What is truth? And how do I find it?

WHAT IS TRUTH?

The truth, as spoken of in John 16:13, refers to a particular body of knowledge by which the believer is to order his or her life. This particular body of knowledge allows the Christian to choose, with complete certainty, an appropriate course of action. This particular body of knowledge brings to the disciple of Jesus Christ a philosophy of thought that can be depended on with absolute reliability. *Truth*, according to the meaning of the word as found in our text, is that particular reservoir of insight that serves as a trustworthy, unfailing foundation for determining an appropriate course of action. *Truth*, according to our Lord, is that designated sphere of reality by which a person can navigate his or her way triumphantly through the obstacles, difficulties, and questions that constantly assault the believer.

THE ORIGIN OF TRUTH

Where does the Holy Spirit get this body of knowledge that serves as the believer's basis of decision making? He gets it from God.

Look at the middle of John 16:13: "He will not speak on His own initiative, but whatever He hears, He will speak." What is the Holy Spirit hearing, or more precisely, to whom is the Holy Spirit listening? Look at John 15:26: "When the Helper comes, whom I will send to you from the Father, that is the Spirit of truth, who proceeds from the Father, He will testify about Me." The Holy Spirit listens to God and speaks nothing more and nothing less than the mind and heart of God. When the Holy Spirit speaks, the Holy Spirit speaks the very words of God Himself. In fact, the Holy Spirit comes from God in such a way that His voice *is* God's voice.

HOW DO I FIND THE TRUTH?

If the Holy Spirit gets this special body of knowledge from God, how does the Holy Spirit get this body of knowledge to me?

Look at the last phrase of John 16:13: "He will disclose to you what is to come." Notice the word translated *disclose*. That word refers to something that is revealed or made visible in a clear, conspicuous way. The Holy Spirit brings the truth — the heart and mind of God – into focus in such a way that I can plainly understand and apply it.

The primary way that the Holy Spirit reveals the heart and mind of God is through the written record of the Bible. Some twenty centuries ago, the Holy Spirit took the knowledge He received from God and worked that knowledge into the minds and hearts of a group of men who would eventually commit that body of knowledge to writing – what we now call the New Testament. Who were these men? The apostles—men whom Jesus chose to be with Him during the years of His earthly ministry, men who would be trained by Him personally, men who would be gifted with the unique capacity of bringing to us the very words of God as revealed by the Holy Spirit. This circle included the original twelve disciples, minus Judas, plus Paul, plus James and Jude—the half brothers of the earthly Jesus.

Beginning with the thirteenth chapter of John, and continuing through the seventeenth chapter, Jesus addressed the men we call apostles. Notice what Jesus said to them:

> The Helper, the Holy Spirit, whom the Father will send in My name, He will teach you all things, and

bring to your remembrance all that I said to you. (John 14:26).

When He, the Spirit of truth, comes, He will guide you into all the truth; for He will not speak on His own initiative, but whatever He hears, He will speak; and He will disclose to you what is to come. He will glorify Me, for He will take of Mine and will disclose it to you. (John 16:13-14)

In John 14:26, Jesus is referring to the gospels; in John 16:13-14, He is referring to the epistles and the Revelation. The apostles may not have understood it that way in the moment that Jesus said it—just as they didn't understand many things in the moment Jesus said them—but reflecting on the words of Jesus, those men could have no doubt as to what He meant, and as we look back on the words of Jesus we should have no doubt. And in the same way the Holy Spirit revealed to the apostles the content of the New Testament, the Holy Spirit also revealed to the ancient prophets the content of the Old Testament.

HOW GOD SEES REALITY

The Holy Spirit has been as plain and as clear as He could possibly be in revealing to us reality as God sees it. The Bible gives us the truth and nothing but the truth. Any spiritual teaching or philosophy of life that runs contrary to the Word of God is to be rejected as unreliable and utterly false.

Amazingly, in a book published by the president of a well-known Christian university, the author plainly states that we are neither to equate the words of the Bible with the words of God, nor are we to see the Bible as our primary source about faith. His statement is a direct denial of everything Jesus says in the verses before us in this chapter.

Let me say that I sincerely hope I would never treat anyone

or anyone's beliefs with disrespect. No one can be open to the gospel if they or their beliefs are treated with malice and ridicule. So, allow me to respectfully yet strongly disagree.

That which is accurately known about God, life, and eternity comes through the Holy Spirit and is revealed in the Bible. If that is not so, then Jesus is a liar. If that is not so, then the Bible is just another book and we are wasting our time. However, if we believe the words of Jesus, then the Bible is not just another book. Rather, the Bible brings to us the thoughts of God Himself—thoughts that are otherwise known as truth, that is, a body of knowledge that serves as a reliable and trustworthy basis for decision making.

STRAIGHT FROM GOD

What kind of decision-making information do we find in this body of knowledge that we call the Bible? First, we find statutes or commandments. They provide authoritative rules of conduct; behavioral rights and wrongs; and divine laws that protect physical health, preserve emotional well-being, and promote peace between God and man as well as between man and man. Further, these laws provide society with moral order. These statutes or commandments can be characterized in five ways:

1. A statute or commandment is narrowly applicable; that is, it speaks to specific circumstances.

2. A statute or commandment is in force at all times and in all places, that is, it is absolute.

3. A statute or commandment is clear-cut. There is no room for misunderstanding. You don't need a spiritual Supreme Court to unravel all the nuances because there are no nuances.

4. A statute or commandment is precise, brief, and to the point.

5. Statutes or commandments are designed to give us either release or restriction. A statute or commandment says, "Do this" (release) or, "Don't do this" (restriction).

Many statutes or commandments are familiar to us:

- "Treat people the same way you want them to treat you" (Matt. 7:12).

- "Then Peter came and said to Him, 'Lord, how often shall my brother sin against me and I forgive him? Up to seven times?' Jesus said to him, 'I do not say to you, up to seven times, but up to seventy times seven'" (Matt. 18:21-22).

- "Never take your own revenge ... but leave room for the wrath of God, for it is written, 'Vengeance is Mine, I will repay,' says the Lord" (Rom. 12:19).

- "This is the will of God ... that you abstain from sexual immorality" (1 Thess. 4:3).

- "You shall not murder. You shall not commit adultery. You shall not steal. You shall not bear false witness" (Ex. 20:13-16).

All these examples come from the heart and mind of God. They tell us what to do and what not to do. They tell us what is always right and what is always wrong. They tell us clearly. They tell us absolutely. They protect us from others. They protect others from us. They promote an orderly and peaceful society whose citizens can live without fear.

ONCE UPON A TIME IN AMERICA

Our nation used to live by the statutes of God. Our nation used to hang the Ten Commandments in the halls of justice. People used to have such a reverence for right and wrong that you could go to the ball game and leave your purse in your seat when you went for refreshments, and you never thought once about whether that purse would be there when you got back. Most everyone used to sleep soundly with their doors unlocked and windows open. Even I can remember those days. My children cannot. Many of your grandchildren cannot. Is it possible that the fear and violence that engulfs our society today is connected to the removal of God's statutes and commandments from our nation's political and educational institutions? In my opinion, there is a direct connection.

Certainly, there are many questions and decisions in life that cannot be answered by statutes and commandments. That is precisely why the Holy Spirit brings to us, in the Word of God, so much more than abbreviated rules of conduct. Yet advanced truth cannot be mastered until simple truth is firmly grasped and applied. What we have been talking about in this chapter may seem more like a course in Human Behavior 101. Some of you may have begun this section hoping to attend a doctoral level course on deep spirituality. You may be saying, "Let's move beyond this curriculum of bonehead discipleship." And we will, but first we must establish the foundation. We must examine the issues of right and wrong that people face on a daily basis.

- Is it okay to sign that check even though it hasn't been authorized?

- Is it okay to file this report even though it has some white lies in it?
- Is it okay to take this equipment home or these supplies home even though I am clearly doing so without permission?
- Is it okay to call in sick even though I'm not sick?
- Is it okay to steal my friend's test answers and claim them as my own?
- Does it really matter if I lie to my parents about where I'm going or where I went?
- What's wrong with having sex before marriage?
- Church is not really important, is it?
- Who cares if a person drinks, smokes, or uses drugs a little?
- Pornography never hurt anybody, did it?
- Am I supposed to treat my sister like I want to be treated?
- What do you mean, "Forgive my husband"? You just don't know how hard he is to get along with.
- If I can't complain and murmur at home, where can I complain and murmur?
- I may have to be patient with my boss, but God can't expect me to be patient with my wife.

THE SIMPLE TRUTH

The Holy Spirit lives in your heart to lead you. That truth may seem mundane and elementary to some. Yet we can no longer assume that everyone who walks through the doors of a church knows the difference between right and wrong. The Holy Spirit leads us, and He leads us first to the behavioral statutes and commandments found in Scripture.

The Holy Spirit Workout #10

FINDING HIS TRUTH EVERY DAY

Each day we make hundreds of decisions, from what to cook for breakfast to how fast to drive to work, to whether we should take the time to kiss our loved one good-bye before hurrying out the door. But rarely do we stop to think that each decision we make reflects some aspect of our underlying value system.

Maybe a low-fat breakfast is the rule in your life because you are committed to honoring God's gift of health. Maybe you leave the road-rage in the trunk because anger and hostility push us away from each other and from God. Maybe your value system regards the love between husband and wife as one of the closest manifestations of God's love on earth, so you always make time to kiss good-bye.

In this workout, you are to write a journal of one day in your life, but focus it on the values that lie beneath each of your decisions and actions. What message about your values are you sending to God and to others with every decision you make?

Example entry:

Action: I made a second pot of coffee immediately after the first and drank it.

Value implication: I seem to have lost sight that coffee is a stimulant and that I am making my body dependent on it. I need to think more about seemingly innocent addictive behaviors and what they say about who and what is in control of my life. Only the Holy Spirit should sit in the seat of control, not caffeine.

Set aside a time and place each day to read the Bible. Keep that time and go to that place often. The Holy Spirit will meet you there, and you will hear the voice of God.

Chapter Eleven

What if Right/Wrong is not the Question?

I have more insight than all my teachers, for Thy testimonies are my meditation. I understand more than the aged, because I have observed Thy precepts.
— Psalm 119:99-100

What you will learn in this chapter:

* Where to find abutments for the soul
* Whether or not you are a bonehead Christian
* Five ways to discover truth in Scripture
* How to hear the voice of God

At one time or another, we've all asked ourselves a question like this one: How will I possibly find my way through these obstacles, difficulties, and problems that assault me? John 16:13 gives the answer: "When He, the Spirit of truth, comes, He will guide you into all the truth."

As a Christian, I navigate my way through the obstacles, difficulties, and problems of life by following the leadership of the

Holy Spirit. Which raises the question: How does the Holy Spirit communicate His leadership? In the previous chapter we learned that the Holy Spirit speaks to us — first and foremost — through the written record of the Bible, in which the heart and mind of God are revealed.

As we look into the pages of the Bible, we also discover statutes and commandments that lead us to know right from wrong. These statutes and commandments are divine laws from the heart and mind of God that set out, unmistakably, appropriate behavior and conduct. These statutes or commandments are in force at all times and in all places. They are clearcut. They are precise. They are designed to give us release (do this) or restriction (don't do this).

However, we need more than statutes and commandments if we are to navigate our way successfully through the maze of obstacles, difficulties, and problems that confront us. Some questions and issues are not a matter of simple, straightforward rules of behavior. That is precisely why, as we follow the leadership of the Holy Spirit, we are led not only to scriptural statutes and commandments, but also to biblical principles and precepts.

ABUTMENTS FOR THE SOUL

Principles and precepts are far-reaching foundational truths that serve as bridge abutments for our moral code, each one supporting large sections of our lives. Principles and precepts are not about the mere gathering or dissemination of data. Principles and precepts are God-given axioms that give us the ability to make sound judgments in complex decisions. They help us distinguish not simply between good and bad, but between better and best. Principles and precepts help us unravel the tangle of life's twists and turns. They help us find practical, commonsense direction in the midst of confusing, mind-boggling difficulties. Principles and precepts share at least five characteristics.

Principles Are Multidimensional

A single principle can be applied to many different scenarios or circumstances. Think of a principle or precept as biblical spandex—one size fits all.

Principles Are General Truths

If followed and applied, these truths create an environment in which a desired result or goal has the best chance of becoming reality. Principles and precepts do not offer bedrock guarantees of specific outcomes like the mathematical formulas *a* plus *b* always equals *c*. Principles and precepts can be affected by unknown, unaccounted for variables. All things being equal, *a* plus *b* will equal *c*, but all things are not always equal. And when they aren't, principles and precepts give us the best opportunity to reach a desired result.

Principles Force Us to Think

In fact, mental and emotional wrestling with a principle or precept may run the course of many hours, if not days or even months. A statute or commandment can be easily understood. The only struggle a commandment or statute requires is the struggle of obedience. However, a principle or precept can compel us to dig deep, to ask personal questions we've never asked before, to face issues we've never faced before, or to confront weaknesses we never knew we had. As a result, principles and precepts can challenge our thought processes in ways we never dreamed they would be challenged.

They Can Require Long-term Commitments

Principles and precepts are not microwave approaches to the dilemmas of life. They are more like crock-pot recipes that call for slow-boil persistence and endurance. Principles and precepts work best over the long haul and thus serve those who see life as an art to be mastered rather than as a daily contest to determine who stands as the current king-of-the-hill.

Principles Result in Spiritual Growth

Why? Because grasping a principle or precept often requires extended periods of study, reflection, and prayer. Not everyone is willing to study, reflect, and pray, but those who are often find those disciplines to be the difference between being grounded with the turkeys or soaring like an eagle.

IN THE HEART OF CORINTH

All five of these characteristics can be found abundantly in a study of 2 Corinthians 6:14-18:

> Do not be bound together with unbelievers; for what partnership have righteousness and lawlessness, or what fellowship has light and darkness? Or what harmony has Christ with Belial, or what has a believer in common with an unbeliever? Or what agreement has the temple of God with idols? For we are the temple of the living God; just as God said, "I will dwell in them and walk among them; and I will be their God, and they shall be my people. Therefore, come out from their midst and be separate," says the Lord. "And do not touch what is unclean; and I will welcome you. And I will be a father to you, and you shall be sons and daughters to Me," says the Lord Almighty.

This passage of Scripture is not for unthinking Christians who want spoon-fed theology and simple commandments. These verses demand more of us. If we are going to glean appropriate insights from this passage and draw healthy, practical conclusions from Paul's writing, then we must work our way to its heart in five distinct stages.

Stage 1: Ask Questions
At first reading, these verses could result in more misunderstanding than understanding. So we must ask some serious questions. For instance, do these verses require the believer to avoid any and all contact with nonbelievers? Are Christians to be isolationists? Suppose that a husband or wife accepts Christ as Lord and Savior but the spouse does not. Are we to infer from these verses that a saved husband or wife should divorce or leave the unsaved spouse?

Stage 2: Compare Scriptures
Those questions lead us to the second stage, which is comparative study. If we compare our study passage to other passages, we may find answers to our initial questions.

For example, we asked: Do these verses from 2 Corinthians require the believer to avoid any and all contact with nonbelievers? Are we to be isolationists?

An answer can be found in Luke 5:29-32:

> Levi gave a big reception for Him in his house; and there was a great crowd of tax collectors and other people who were reclining at the table with them. The Pharisees and their scribes began grumbling at His disciples, saying, "Why do you eat and drink with the tax collectors and sinners?" And Jesus answered and said to them, "It is not those who are well who need a physician, but those who are sick. I have not come to call the righteous but sinners to repentance."

This story tells us that Jesus intentionally associated with sinners for the purpose of winning them to the Kingdom. Jesus had to be with them to win them. Jesus did not belittle those who were immoral and self-centered; He befriended them. Jesus did not avoid the sinner but worked to attract the sinner. Since this story is also contained in Matthew and Mark, we might say that it holds triple significance for the Christian, and we would do well to follow Christ's example. Therefore, Paul cannot possibly be telling us in 2 Corinthians 6:14-18 to avoid any and all contact with nonbelievers.

We also asked: Are we to infer from 2 Corinthians 6:14-18 that a saved husband or wife should divorce or leave the unsaved spouse?

Again, we profit from a comparative study. Here is 1 Corinthians 7:12-16:

> If any brother has a wife who is an unbeliever, and she consents to live with him, he must not divorce her. And a woman who has an unbelieving husband, and he consents to live with her, she must not send her husband away. For the unbelieving husband is sanctified through his wife, and the unbelieving wife is sanctified through her believing husband; for otherwise your children are unclean, but now they are holy. Yet if the unbelieving one leaves, let him leave; the brother or sister is not under bondage in such cases, but God has called us to peace. For how do you know, O wife, whether you will save your husband? Or how do you know, O husband, whether you will save your wife?

What does Paul say to a believing spouse about an unbelieving spouse? Use your marital relationship as an opportunity to win your unbelieving husband or wife to the Lord. There are other passages we could use for comparison, but for the moment, using comparative study we have answered the second question: A Christian husband or wife should not seek to divorce or leave a non-Christian spouse as long as the spouse is willing to remain in the relationship.

Stage 3: Gather Background

Our third step is to learn something about the historical backdrop of Paul's writing to the Christians of ancient Corinth. You can purchase a good commentary on Paul's letters to the church at Corinth, or, if you have a study Bible, you can look at the introductory material found at the beginning of each book in your Bible.[1] The introductory section in my study Bible says this about Corinth:

> The city was filled with shrines and temples, but the most prominent was the Temple of Aphrodite... . Worshipers of the "goddess of love" made free use of the (Temple's) 1,000 consecrated prostitutes... . This cosmopolitan center thrived on ... entertainment, vice, and corruption; pleasure-seekers came there to spend money on a holiday from morality. Corinth became so notorious for its evils that the term ... ("to act like a Corinthian") became a synonym for debauchery and prostitution.[2]

Gathering historical background, we learn that those who lived in Corinth had a reputation of rampant immorality. Whether or not a person was actually immoral, he or she was considered immoral by outsiders simply by being a citizen of this city. The background also signals to us that those who stood for the good and the right were clearly in the minority. The forces of evil dominated Corinthian culture, and those dark energies could easily swallow up anyone who desired to be different. Living a life of consistent Christianity was a difficult task in ancient Corinth.

Stage 4: Study the Words

As we look at this passage we discover three sets of significant ideas.

- Category 1: Union — *bound together with, partnership, fellowship, harmony, in common with, agreement.* These terms refer to symphony, to concert, to synchronization, to having the same goals, to reaching for the same objectives, to going the same direction, to drawing water from the same well, to playing from the same score of music, to following the same leader, to strapping oneself into a harness with a like-minded person. The words suggest a well-fitted, close-knit association.

- Category 2: Disunion — *righteousness and lawlessness, light and darkness, Christ and Belial, believer and unbeliever, temple of God and idols, come out, be separate, do not touch.* These phrases depict things that are not merely opposite, but things that have absolutely no hope of harmonious connection, things that can never be rightly related, things that are impossible to join together with success, things that can in no way or under any circumstances mix — and to try is an operation of utter futility.

- Category 3: Communion — *we are the temple of the living God, I will dwell in them, I will walk among them, I will be their God, they shall be My people, I will be a father to you, you shall be sons and daughters to Me.* What kind of images do those phrases paint? I see a picture of intimacy and shared purpose. I see a picture of unified family, the lesser depending upon the greater. I see a picture of children inheriting and expressing the traits of their father. I see a picture of power and blessing.

Stage 5: Apply to Your Life

Now it is time to bring this passage from the past to the present and let it live in our lives. After working through the first four stages you can finally ask: What does 2 Corinthians 6:14-18 mean for me today?

First, the passage means that we have an intimate connection with God. God is present in our lives, and our allegiance is to Him and to Him alone. It means that His life is to be distinctly reflected in our lives.

Second, it means that we belong to a family of men and women who also have an intimate connection to God. There are men and women in this world who—because of that shared connection with God—think like we think, say what we say, and do what we do. It means that there are those who share our goals, understand our vision, and dream our dreams. It means there are those who are going where we are going. It means that there are those who are reading the same map, who hold to the same values, and who are guided by the same beliefs.

Third, 2 Corinthians 6:14-18 means that if we want the best chance at knowing a life that is filled with meaning, a life that is effective for the Kingdom, a life that is satisfying to the end, then we are to reserve our most intimate and contractual relationships for those who are our spiritual brothers and sisters.

What does this mean for a Christian man who wants to ask an unbelieving woman for a date? What does this mean for the teenager? Girls, should a date with a non-Christian boy even be accepted? I'm not telling you the answer. Let the principle tell you the answer. Wrestle with the principle, not with me. However, I will tell you this in the strongest of terms: Ignore the principle and the consequences could be unimaginable. I commonly counsel those who have ignored this principle in the past and are now paying the price. Remember, the principles and precepts of God give you solid ground to stand on in the future.

What does 2 Corinthians 6:14-18 say about business relationships? What kind of partners should you look for? What kind of corporations should you be contractually connected to? I once said to a man: "If I'm a man of integrity, I don't work for the people you work for. I don't represent those who lie. I don't represent those who deceive. I don't represent those whose words today cannot be trusted tomorrow."

What does 2 Corinthians 6:14-18 say about close friendships? Friendship is one thing, but what if friendship begins leading to compromise? Do not be naïve—friendships can quickly overwhelm and outflank you.

What does 2 Corinthians 6:14-18 say about choices of entertainment? What if going to certain places or being involved in certain things tarnishes our reputations as sons and daughters of God? Most certainly, if we learn anything from this passage we learn that a clearly distinctive lifestyle is paramount to our identity as Christians. If a person is not strong enough to say no to a friend, then the friendship should be abandoned. If a particular environment causes a person to slip, that person should get out of that environment immediately. We are not to be evangelists at the expense of purity and devotion.

TO HEAR THE VOICE OF GOD

Is the truth of 2 Corinthians 6:14-18 multidimensional? Absolutely. I'm not sure that we've even scratched the surface. Is the truth of this passage a guarantee? No. You can marry a Christian and still end in divorce. You can go into business with a Christian and still get cheated. You can share your deepest feelings with a Christian friend and still find yourself betrayed. Yet your best chance is with someone who dearly loves the Lord.

Do these verses make you think? Deeper than you ever wish to think. Would adherence to this passage make you grow spiritually? Yes, taller than you've ever grown.

At the beginning of this chapter, I suggested that the primary purpose of the Holy Spirit is to lead us, and that the Holy Spirit speaks to us through the written record of the Bible. Yes, there are other ways that the Holy Spirit speaks to us, and we're going to talk about them all. However, before He speaks to us any other way, He speaks to us through the pages of Scripture. In those pages, the Holy Spirit reveals to us the heart and mind of God. If we will not follow His leadership there, He will not lead us anywhere.

What am I asking you to do? I'm asking you to follow the leadership of the Spirit to the Bible. Open the Scripture on a regular basis. Spend time in the Word and hear what the Spirit reveals about the mind and heart of God. Get an easy-to-read, translation that is a study Bible. Set aside a time and place. Keep that time and go to that place often.

The Holy Spirit will meet you there, and you will hear the voice of God.

NOTES

[1] Get an accurate, modern language translation (not a paraphrase) of the Bible. My first suggestion is the New American Standard Version in the Ryrie Study Bible Edition, or the Zondervan Bible, or the New Life Application Bible. My second suggestion is the New King James Version in the Believer's Study Bible Edition. Each of these provides introductory material to all the books, as well as accompanying comments or studies.

² First Corinthians: Introduction, (NASV: The Open Bible, Expanded Edition: 1985), 1,146.

The Holy Spirit Workout #11

TRAVELING THE PRINCIPLED ROAD

The road can be long and rough. It can be filled with confusing twists and turns, potholed with temptations, and barricaded by hardship. But if the Holy Spirit walks with us, if we seek and follow His leadership, the principles and precepts of Christendom can provide guideposts, mile markers, and all the exit signs we need during our journey to truth on this earth.

Exercise 1

Think of a recent life situation in which you applied a biblical principle or precept. What difference did it make in the outcome?

The situation:

The principle or precept:

The outcome:

Exercise 2

To hear God, we must first be listening. Do you have a time and place to hear God through His written Word? If the answer is no, take a pencil right now and list the times when you can make a regular commitment to read and discuss Scripture. You might include a time you can get together with someone else, perhaps a family member, to discuss Scripture.

Then the cloud covered the tent of meeting, and the glory of the Lord filled the tabernacle. Moses was not able to enter the tent of meeting because the cloud had settled on it, and the glory of the Lord filled the tabernacle. And throughout all their journeys whenever the cloud was taken up from over the tabernacle, the sons of Israel would set out; but if the cloud was not taken up, then they did not set out until the day when it was taken up. For throughout all their journeys, the cloud was on the tabernacle by day, and there was fire in it by night, in the sight of all the house of Israel.

—

Exodus 40:34-38

Chapter Twelve

When the Bible Doesn't Give the Answers

How does the Holy Spirit lead us when the Bible doesn't have the answer? Through impressions of the heart.

What you will learn in this chapter:

* God's true dwelling place
* How to get answers from God
* God's non-vocal communications
* Six keys to opening your heart to God

Where do you meet with God? Ancient Israel, while still a struggling infant nation, met with God at the tent of meeting. Otherwise known as the tabernacle, the tent of meeting was a portable sanctuary that served as God's house or dwelling place among His people. It also served as a point of rendezvous. Anyone seeking a personal encounter with the Lord sought that encounter at the tent of meeting. The verses from Exodus provide us three key insights.

First, the ancient Israelites were a people on the move. "And throughout all their journeys whenever the cloud was taken up from over the tabernacle, the sons of Israel would set out... For throughout all their journeys, the cloud was on the tabernacle by day, and there was fire in it by night, in the sight of all the house of Israel" (Ex. 40:36-38).

Notice the repeated phrase *all their journeys*. Note the word translated *journeys*. In the story of Israel's exodus from Egypt, this word—or some form of this word—appears sixty-seven times, suggesting that the people of Israel—at least in the early stages of their development—were extremely nomadic. They didn't stay in one place very long. Israel moved, and moved often.

The second insight is that God made His presence known to them. "For throughout all their journeys, the cloud was on the tabernacle by day, and there was fire in it by night, in the sight of all the house of Israel" (Ex. 40:38).

Note the phrase *in the sight of all the house of Israel*. The people of Israel kept a constant watch on the tabernacle, especially the cloud that covered the tabernacle by day and the fire that glowed from the tabernacle by night. Why? The cloud and the fire represented the presence of God.

Where I grew up, you knew somebody was home in the daytime because the front door was open, and you knew somebody was home at night because the porch light was on. If the door was closed or the light was off, you didn't bother knocking—no one was home. For Israel, the cloud was like an open door in the day, and the fire was like a porch light in the night. The cloud and the fire let the people know that God was at home and that His home was with them.

Third, the Israelites mirrored God. "And throughout all their journeys whenever the cloud was taken up from over the tabernacle, the sons of Israel would set out; but if the cloud was not taken up, then they did not set out until the day when it was taken up" (Ex. 40:36-37).

Not only do the words *set out* appear twice in these verses, the phrase can be found 160 times in the Old Testament, and most of the time in the stories of the Exodus.

Literally, the words *set out* mean to pull the tent pegs, that is, to break camp. The Israelites packed up and moved out hundreds of times, but they never did so unless the cloud packed up and moved out first. As long as that cloud stayed put, they stayed put. They did not move one inch unless that cloud moved one inch ahead of them. They went where God went. They camped where God camped. If He moved to the right, they moved to the right. If he moved to the left, they moved to the left. If He stopped, they stopped. If He rested, they rested. They became a mirror of God's activities. If you wanted to know where God happened to be, you looked at Israel. If you wanted to know what God was up to, you looked at Israel.

THE TABERNACLE WITHIN

What does this story mean for us today? First, God still inhabits His tabernacle. The glory of the Lord still fills His dwelling place. However, the tabernacle God inhabits today is not a house made of animal skins and wooden posts. Neither is His dwelling place a building constructed of brick and mortar. The church you worship in Sunday after Sunday is not God's residence. Yes, His people meet there and He meets with His people as they come together to celebrate their relationship with Him. We are not wrong in referring to these localities as the tent of meeting, but those buildings are not where God dwells.

Buildings are not God's tabernacle — you are God's dwelling place. If you have received Jesus Christ as Lord and Savior, then God literally inhabits your body. First Corinthians 6:19 says, "Do you not know that your body is a temple (habitation, house, sanctuary) of the Holy Spirit who is in you?"

You may wonder why I keep bring up this idea that God resides in our bodies. It's because I can't get over it. I'm still trying to come to terms with the idea of *God in me*. I know that *God in me* is true, not false. I know that *God in me* is fact, not fiction. I accept that God is in me—but taking it all in is another matter.

If you find the glory of God filling that ancient wilderness tabernacle to be wondrous and miraculous, then think about the glory of God filling your body and your life. When we cross the biblical bridge from then to now, that is exactly what we discover. You are the wondrous, miraculous tabernacle of God.

We discover something else, too. Not only are you the tabernacle of God, but you can actually discern the movement of God in your life. Like the Israelites, you and I are to keep our eyes constantly on God. When He moves, we move. When He stops, we stop. When He goes to the right, we go to the right. When He goes to the left, we go to the left. Our motion is to be a mirror of His motion. We do what we see Him doing.

This means that God tells us exactly what He wants us to do. It means that God reveals His precise will to us in the decision-making process. It means that in every circumstance I can know and do—not what I think is best—but what God thinks is best. It means that even when the Bible does not give the answer I can still get an answer from God.

Sounds great, doesn't it? There's only one catch. How do I know what God is doing? How do I see the movement of God? How do I discern when God goes to the right or when He goes to the left? How do I determine what God thinks is best? How do I hear God's answers?

ANSWERS STRAIGHT FROM GOD

That's the essential question of this chapter: When the Bible doesn't have the answer, how do I get the answer from God? We have already learned that the Holy Spirit lives in our bodies, and that the Holy Spirit has been given to us by God to lead us. In fact, that is the Holy Spirit's primary purpose—to lead us. We have already learned that the Holy Spirit leads us, first, by revealing God's Word and giving us the ability to understand and apply the truth of Scripture. That is referred to by some as "scriptural revelation," and it is produced by the Holy Spirit.

But what if the Bible doesn't give the answer? For instance, the Bible can tell me what kind of person I should marry, but the Bible doesn't tell me precisely whom I should marry. Most important, as a Christian, I am to marry another Christian. As a Christian, I am to marry a woman who is deeply in love with the Lord Jesus Christ. That much is clear from Scripture. However, there are lots of Christian women who are deeply in love with Jesus, but which one is the one for me?

There are many questions the Bible does not answer. We face all kinds of choices and decisions that require more than what the Bible gives us.

- Where should I work?
- Where should I live?
- Where should I go to church?
- Where should I go to school, and what should my major be?
- What organizations should I join?
- How should I divide my time between spouse, children, and personal recreation?
- Should I teach this class?
- Should I accept this position?
- Should I run for political office?
- Is now the right time to share my faith with this person, and precisely how should he or she be approached?
- Should I take this promotion and move my family to another state?

In 1994, when the congregation of First Baptist Church in Brunswick, Georgia, asked me to come serve as their pastor, there were two other churches asking us to do the same—one in Alabama and one in Texas. We could have as easily gone west, but we went southeast. In doing so, we believed then and believe now that we followed God's movement to Brunswick. How did we make that decision? Not by finding a verse in the Bible. But wait a minute! If the Bible does not give the answer, am I on my own? If the Holy Spirit leads me, does He lead me only as far as the Bible and no more? Absolutely not.

Yes, the Holy Spirit leads us first to the Bible. We follow the Holy Spirit to the Word of God before we follow Him anywhere else. However, the leadership of the Holy Spirit does not stop with the Bible. When necessary, the leadership of the Holy Spirit takes us beyond the Bible. When the Bible doesn't have the answer, then the Holy Spirit leads us beyond scriptural revelation to extrabiblical revelation.

EXTRABIBLICAL DOESN'T MEAN EXTRACONTRARY

Having said that, let me caution you to remember that when the Holy Spirit leads us beyond the Bible, the Holy Spirit never leads us contrary to the Bible. For example, if you, as a Christian, marry someone who is not a Christian, don't credit that decision to the leadership of the Holy Spirit. Why? Because the Bible says, "Do not be bound together with unbelievers." Another example, if you, as a Christian, are treated unjustly and you decide to respond to that injustice with an injustice of your own, don't pacify your act of vengeance by thinking that God will understand. Why? Because the Bible says, "Love your enemies, do good to those who hate you, bless those who curse you, pray for those who mistreat you." You will never see God moving in a way that is contrary to His Word. The Holy Spirit will never lead you to any act or decision that violates the commandments or principles of Scripture.

A DEEP, INNER KNOWING

With that in mind, how does the Holy Spirit lead us when the Bible doesn't have the answer? Through impressions of the heart. There are those who say that God speaks to them audibly. I must confess that I've never heard God's voice in an audible way—at least, not that I know about. I know that Moses did. I know that Peter, James, and John did. I know that Paul did. I'm not saying that God can't speak in an audible voice, or that He won't speak in an audible voice. I'm simply saying that — as far as I know — God has never spoken to me audibly. I have no doubt that He has communicated with me in a clear, unmistakable fashion. However, that communication has come through impressions of the heart. No smoke, no fire like that of ancient Israel — but impressions of the heart. Not seeing and hearing physically, but seeing and hearing spiritually. I'm talking about a deep inner knowing.

I don't want to sound too mystical here, but there is a mystical dimension about it. Mystical in that these impressions come at different times and in different ways. For me, these impressions of the heart sometimes come in the middle of the night. For no apparent reason, I'll wake up and my mind will be consumed with a particular impression that tells me exactly what to do in some specific situation and exactly how to do it. Sometimes these impressions will come as I'm spending time alone before God. Sometimes they will come in the midst of a meeting, and though I'm surrounded by hundreds or thousands of people, it's not the voice outside but the voice inside that's ringing in my ears.

Impressions of the heart.

You don't know when or where they will come. You also don't know how they will come. Sometimes, these impressions come as an inexplicable peace that settles over my mind and heart—a peace, yes; a peace, no; a peace to do this or a peace not to do that. Other times, these impressions come as a terrible troubling that shakes my mind and heart—a troubling, yes; a troubling, no; a troubling to do this or a troubling not to do that. Sometimes these impressions are like a gentle whisper or a distant thunder, and sometimes they are like a gigantic shout or the roar of a lion. Sometimes these impressions come instantaneously and without strain. Other times they come slowly and with great struggle.

Impressions of the heart—that is how the Spirit leads us beyond the Bible.

OPENING YOUR HEART TO GOD

Here are six keys that have helped me and I hope will help you receive and recognize the speaking of God through impressions of the heart.

Simply Ask

Ask God to lead you. Ask God to speak to you. Ask God to communicate with you. Ask God to reveal His movement for your life. James 4:2 says, "You do not have because you do not ask."

Ask and Believe

Believe that God will speak to you. Believe that God *wants to* reveal Himself to you. Believe that God is longing to let you know what He is doing in your life. Do not doubt, do not waver, but constantly anticipate. Start out every day expecting a word from God. James 1:5-6 says, "If any of you lacks wisdom, let him ask of God ... but he must ask in faith without any doubting."

Ask with Right Motive

What is the right motive? The glorification of God. Here is what Mike Fleischmann wrote in *Discipleship Journal*:

> We must carefully weigh our requests against the Kingdom purposes of God... [God is not to be] viewed as a great big vending machine in the sky [where you] pick whatever you would like and push the button... God's ultimate concern is not with our team winning its ball game, but in Himself being glorified in our ball game. His ultimate concern is not that we all have perfect health, but that we lift up every ounce of our health to His honor. His ultimate concern is not that we have a high-paying job ... but that we praise Him for what He provides. His ultimate concern is that we are consumed with His glory ....[1]

As James 4: 3 says, "You ask and do not receive, because you ask with wrong motives, so that you may spend it on your pleasures."

Ask with a Clean Heart

Confess sin. Forsake lifestyle sin. Make yourself available to whatever God wants. When things are going well between my children and me, I am more likely to give them what they are asking for. Is it any different with God? Isaiah 59:2 says, "Your iniquities have made a separation between you and your God, and your sins have hidden His face from you so that He does not hear."

Ask Persistently and with Patience

Don't give up and don't give out. There are times when God makes us wait. There are times when we must wrestle and struggle as a necessary part of our training and maturity. Decisions with long-term implications often take longer. Deciphering flesh from Spirit and impulse from insight is not always easy. Matthew 7:7 says, "Ask (keep on asking), and it will be given to you; seek (keep on seeking), and you will find; knock (keep on knocking)," and it will be opened to you."

Ask with Body and Mind Rested

Chronic fatigue will kill a person's sensitivity to the Holy Spirit as fast as it will kill the romance in a marriage. I'm not saying that God will never speak to you in the midst of mental and physical fatigue, but hearing Him is so much more difficult through tired ears. Rest is a vital part of knowing God intimately.

NOTE

[1] Mike Fleischmann, "Prayer Blockers: Why Many of Our Prayers Are Never Answered," *Discipleship Journal* 97 (Jan/Feb 1997): 46.

The Holy Spirit Workout #12

FINDING THE TABERNACLE WITHIN

The Israelites of Exodus knew what God was doing by keeping an ever-vigilant eye upon His wilderness tabernacle. Their every movement was a mirror of God's. Today, we are challenged to also follow God, to allow the Holy Spirit to fill our inner tabernacle, to actively seek answers to life's questions through the Scripture and through the extrabiblical revelation God provides as He speaks to our hearts.

Exercise 1

Have you ever had a divinely inspired impression placed upon your heart? First describe the question or dilemma that you were seeking extra-biblical guidance for. Then describe the occasion when you felt in your heart that God had spoken to you.

Exercise 2

Referring back to the six keys listed at the end of this chapter, list the ones of most importance to you in bringing about this communication with God.

The problem many of us face is how to tell the difference between a physical drive and a spiritual desire. Both seem to come from the heart. The answer lies in ... three questions and four attitudes

Chapter Thirteen

Drives *of the* Flesh, Desires *of the* Spirit

*The lust of the flesh and the lust of the eyes and the boastful
pride of life is not from the Father but is from the world.*
— 1 John 2:16

What you will learn in this chapter:

* The red flags of lust
* Connell's 3 + 4 formula for the heart
* The lesson of Samson
* How to avoid a tragedy of the flesh

You are the tabernacle of God. In the moment you became a
disciple of Jesus Christ, your body—literally and actually—became the dwelling place of God. Not only are you the tabernacle of God, but you can discern the movement of God for your
life. You can determine His precise will for the choices and decisions you face every day.

When necessary, the Holy Spirit leads us beyond scriptural
revelation to extrabiblical revelation, often in the form of impressions of the heart. The Holy Spirit communicates with us

through impressions that rise from deep within the inner self—impressions that push us or lead us in certain directions and to certain actions.

Now, I'm not talking about physical drives or natural impulses. Without doubt, both have been designed by God. They are meant to be healthy emotions and inclinations. However, physical drives and natural impulses can easily rage out of control so that they dominate, enslave, and destroy—not only ourselves but others. For that reason, we are to be led by the desires of the Spirit, and those desires come to us through heartfelt impressions.

However, the problem many of us may face is that of telling the difference between a drive of the physical man and a desire of the Spirit. They both seem to come from the heart, springing forth from the inner reaches of our lives. So how do we distinguish between the two? How do we know if an impression of the heart is based in the physical or the spiritual?

CAUTION: FLESH TRAPS AHEAD

Look at 1 John 2:16: "The lust of the flesh and the lust of the eyes and the boastful pride of life, is not from the Father." In this verse we are given three bright red caution signs that a heartfelt impression may be rooted in the physical rather than the spiritual.

- Caution Sign #1: My body wants it (the lust of the flesh).
- Caution Sign #2: My eyes want it (the lust of the eyes).
- Caution Sign #3: My ego wants it (the boastful pride of life).

I use the term *caution signs* because the wants of my body, eyes, and ego are an inherent part of my being. They are necessary elements in the human equation—elements that are meant to serve our highest good. They are meant to have a positive impact on each of us individually and, in turn, have a positive impact on the society in which we live. Without the wants of my body, the wants of my eyes, and the wants of my ego, I would likely not survive. If I did survive, I would not likely achieve, and if I did achieve, I would not likely achieve anything beyond the mediocre and mundane.

However, the wants of my body, my eyes, and my ego can rise to such overpowering heights that they are no longer my servants but become my master—and I their slave. The wants of my body, my eyes, and my ego can become so engaging that I am no longer in command of them but they are in command of me.

Ask yourself these three questions:
1. Does it feel good?
2. Does it look good?
3. Does it advance my personal status?

Now, add these four attitudes:
1. I won't wait to get it.
2. I am willing to violate God's Word to get it.
3. I will take the path of least resistance to get it.
4. I will get it even if others are damaged or destroyed in the process.

Take any of the three questions alone, and the impression of your heart may be all right. Yet, if any one of the three questions can be connected to any one of the four attitudes, then you've got an explosive formula that may ultimately rock your life and the lives of those around you. Chances are, your impression is a dangerous physical drive rather than a spiritual desire. Reject it at once!

SAMSON: APPLYING THE FORMULA

Let's practice applying the formula to the Old Testament character Samson, who stands as a powerful example of the struggle between the physical and the spiritual that we've been discussing. Judges 13:24-25 tells us that God blessed Samson greatly and that, in fact, the Holy Spirit had begun to move upon his life.

However, we fast forward to chapter 14 and discover that Samson did not always know the difference between impressions of the heart as produced by the Spirit and impressions of the heart as produced by his physical drives:

> Then Samson went down to Timnah and saw a woman in Timnah, one of the daughters of the Philistines. So he came back and told his father and mother, "I saw a woman in Timnah, one of the daughters of the Philistines; now therefore, get her for me as a wife." Then his father and his mother said to him, "Is there no woman among the daughters of your relatives, or among all our people, that you go to take a wife from the uncircumcised Philistines?" But Samson said to his father, "Get her for me, for she looks good to me" (Judg. 14: 1-3).

Not only did Samson want to get married, but he based his decision for marriage solely upon physical beauty. In verse 3 he says to his father, "Get her for me, for she looks good to me!" Now, folks, there's certainly nothing wrong with that. Most all of us were drawn to our mates—at least in the beginning—because we thought he or she looked good. No doubt about it: physical attraction is an important part of our romantic relationships.

Indeed, Samson's impression of the heart said to him: *She looks good; ask her to marry you.* I can't fault him for wanting to marry a beautiful woman. To this point, his inclination is okay. However, let's check his attitude. Verse 2 tells us that this woman was a Philistine, and that is precisely what led to a kind of semi-explosion from his mother and father in the third verse. God had expressly forbidden an Israeli from taking wedding vows with anyone who was not also an Israeli, and especially anyone whose beliefs did not center on Jehovah-God. What does this tell us about Samson's attitude? It tells us that Samson was willing to violate God's Word in order to fulfill his inclination.

There's more. Notice what Samson says to his father in verse 2: "Get her for me!" He repeats his desire in verse 3, "Get her for me!" In both verses, the word translated *get* is in the imperative tense—the tense of command. Someone has said that Samson is, no doubt, speaking to his father through clinched teeth. He is not asking; he is demanding! Get her for me! What does that tell us about Samson's attitude? He was not willing to wait. His parents pleaded with him to take time to search among his own people, to move slower, to give this desire plenty of room to mature. But Samson wanted this Philistine woman, and he wanted her now!

The question "Does it look good?" coupled with the attitudes "I won't wait to get it" and "I'm willing to violate God's Word to get it," reveals that Samson's impressions of the heart were based in the physical rather than the spiritual. Thus, unavoidable trouble lay ahead. Should we be surprised that Samson was ultimately betrayed by this woman who he unthinkingly demanded to have as his own?

Before we leave Samson, let's look at verse 4, "However, his father and mother did not know that it was of the LORD, for He was seeking an occasion against the Philistines. Now at that time the Philistines were ruling over Israel." Now, it sounds as if Samson is acting upon God's express will, doesn't it? It seems that way, but I disagree for three reasons. First, God is not going to contradict Himself. Already God had commanded his followers to refrain from marrying anyone outside Israel's faith. Why would God make an exception for Samson or anyone else? He would not. Second, Samson was a Nazarite. That means he had devoted himself completely to the Lord, and that devotion included the kind of woman he would eventually marry. Even if Samson was willing to dishonor his vows as a Nazarite, God would not join him in that dishonor.

Third, the verb translated *was*, in the phrase, *it was of the Lord*, does not appear in the Hebrew text. The literal reading is, "His father and mother did not know *it* of the Lord." The word translated *it* is a demonstrative pronoun that requires the reader to supply a verb. Many translations supply a verb that makes God appear responsible for Samson's demand to marry a pagan woman. One translation says, "This was the Lord's leading." Another translation says, "The Lord was behind the request." However, I don't see it that way. God was not responsible for Samson's demand. The way I see it is that God used His creative sovereignty to produce His ultimate will in spite of Samson's poor choice. One commentator says of verse 4:

> This does not mean that [Samson's parents] were wrong to object to [his] desires and action. Nor does it mean that Samson's desires were virtuous or that his bull-headedness was right. It means that neither Samson's foolishness nor his stubbornness is going to prevent [God] from accomplishing "his" design. [God] can and will use the sinfulness or stupidity of his servants ... for bringing his will to pass.[1]

God accomplished His will regarding the Philistines not because of Samson, but in spite of him.

THE TRAGEDY OF ACHAN

Consider one more example of how our 3 + 4 formula can help distinguish between a desire rooted solely in the physical as opposed to one guided by the Spirit. This example is taken from the book of Joshua, which records Israel's conquest of Canaan. Before we look at verses in chapter 7, some background information is necessary.

In Joshua 6, Israel faced and defeated the city of Jericho—a tremendous victory wrought by the miraculous hand of God against a powerful enemy. Prior to the battle, God told Joshua to warn the warriors of Israel that all the plunder of Jericho belonged to the treasury of the Lord, that none of the bounty was to be kept for themselves:

> The city shall be under the ban, it and all that is in it belongs to the Lord ... As for you, only keep yourselves from the things under the ban, so that you do not covet them and take some of the things under the ban, and make the camp of Israel accursed and bring trouble on it. But all the silver and gold and articles of bronze and iron are holy to the Lord; they shall go into the treasury of the Lord. (Josh. 6: 17a, 18-19)

As chapter 7 opens, Israel is about to do battle with the lowly town of Ai. Victory would surely be easy. However, instead of victory, Israel fell in defeat. It was like winning the Super Bowl one week and then getting beat the next week by a team from the Pee Wee League. Not only that, but thirty-six of Israel's soldiers lost their lives, all providers for their families—husbands, fathers, and sons. The entire nation of Israel groaned in despair. "The men of Ai struck down about thirty-six of their men, and pursued them from the gate as far as Shebarim and struck them down on the descent, so the hearts of the people melted and became as water" (Josh. 7:5).

Why the humiliating defeat? The answer comes in verses 11-12 and 15 of the same chapter:

> Israel has sinned, and they have also transgressed My covenant which I command them. And they have even taken some of the things under the ban and have both stolen and deceived. Moreover, they have also put them among their own things. Therefore the sons of Israel cannot stand before their enemies; they turn their backs before their enemies, for they have become accursed. I will not be with you anymore unless you destroy the things under the ban from your midst ... It shall be that the one who is taken with the things under the ban shall be burned with fire, he and all that belongs to him, because he has transgressed the covenant of the Lord, and because he has committed a disgraceful thing in Israel.

The tragedy comes full circle in verses 19-26:

> Joshua said to Achan, "My son, I implore you, give glory to the Lord, the God of Israel, and give praise to Him; and tell me now what you have done. Do not hide if from me." So Achan answered Joshua and said, "Truly, I have sinned against the Lord, the God of Israel, and this is what I did: when I saw among the spoil a beautiful mantle from Shinar and two hundred shekels of silver and a bar of gold fifty shekels in weight, then I coveted them and took them; and behold, they are concealed in the earth inside my tent with the silver underneath it." So Joshua sent messen-

gers, and they ran to the tent; and behold, it was concealed in his tent with the silver underneath it. They took them from inside the tent and brought them to Joshua and to all the sons of Israel, and they poured them out before the Lord.

Then Joshua and all Israel with him, took Achan the son of Zerah, the silver, the mantle, the bar of gold, his sons, his daughters, his oxen, his donkeys, his sheep, his tent and all that belonged to him; and they brought them up to the valley of Achor. Joshua said, "Why have you troubled us? The Lord will trouble you this day." And all Israel stoned them with stones; and they burned them with fire after they had stoned them with stones. They raised over him a great heap of stones that stands to this day, and the Lord turned from the fierceness of His anger.

Why did Achan take this beautiful imported coat, as well as the silver and gold? Because his heart told him to take them. He had a heartfelt impression that he should have these things for himself. Was his impression a drive of the physical or a desire of the Spirit? To answer this question, we need only to return to our three questions. Does it feel good? Does it look good? Does it advance my personal status?

Certainly, it looked good, this *beautiful mantle*. But most at play was the third question: Will it advance my personal status? Achan's answer would probably sound a bit like this: "Yes! It will make me rich. It will make me the envy of Israel. It will provide for me and my family for years to come."

What about the four attitudes? All four seem to inform Achan's fateful decision. I will not wait to get rich. I will violate God's Word to get rich. I will take the easy road to get rich. I will get rich even if it means damaging and destroying others in the process.

Is there anything wrong with wealth? No, unless my drive for wealth makes me impatient, or causes me to lose integrity, trample on personal discipline, or ignore compassion. Achan's impression of the heart did all four.

What is in your heart today? What is that inner voice urging upon you? Where is that deep-down impression leading you? Is it a drive of the physical, or a desire of the Spirit? Ask three questions:

1. Does it feel good?
2. Does it look good?
3. Does it advance my personal status?

Then check the four attitudes:
1. I won't wait to get it.
2. I will violate God's Word to get it.
3. I will take the path of least resistance to get it.
4. I will get it even if others are damaged or destroyed in the process.

And, most of all, listen to what God tells you in your heart.

NOTE

[1] Dale Ralph Davis, *Such a Great Salvation: Expositions of the Book of Judges* (Grand Rapids: Baker Book House, 1990), p.171.

The Holy Spirit Workout #13

COLLISIONS OF FLESH AND SPIRIT

Our desires can drive us to great heights of achievement. But the dark side of physical drives is their ability to blind our spiritual and moral judgment, a blindness that can lead us and those who love us to destruction. The stories of Samson and Achan make clear the danger of letting ourselves be guided by physical impulses. This chapter also presents a method to help us distinguish between the drives of the flesh and desires of the Spirit.

Have you ever pushed forward in obtaining something even though you knew doing so violated God's desire for your life in that moment? Use the 3 + 4 method outlined below to analyze what happened.

Exercise 1

Reread 1 John 2:16: "The lust of the flesh and the lust of the eyes and the boastful pride of life, is not from the Father." Which of the three caution signs should have lighted up for you?

- Caution Sign #1: My body wants it (the lust of the flesh).
- Caution Sign #2: My eyes want it (the lust of the eyes).
- Caution Sign #3: My ego wants it (the boastful pride of life).

Exercise 2

As we learned, any one of the three cautions by itself is not necessarily a problem, so long as it isn't connected to one of the four attitudes. That combination produces a formula for spiritual abandonment and leads a dangerous physical drive. In this exercise, identify any of the four attitudes that came into play for you.

- Attitude #1. I won't wait to get it.
- Attitude #2. I will violate God's Word to get it.
- Attitude #3. I will take the path of least resistance to get it.
- Attitude #4. I will get it even if others are damaged or destroyed in the process.

Exercise 3

Hindsight, especially spiritual hindsight, is always 20-20. Reflect on your experience and explain what path you wish you had taken in light of the 3 + 4 formula.

THE POWER FOR *L*IVING LIBRARY

PART FOUR

What They Said

One afternoon as we rode together, he shocked me by saying, "You've got everything you need as a preacher except one thing. You need to speak in tongues."

Chapter Fourteen

Tongues: Clearing Away the Rubble

They were all filled with the Holy Spirit and began to speak with other tongues, as the Spirit was giving them utterance.
– Acts 2:4

What you will learn in this chapter:

* The controversial nature of tongues
* What tongues are not
* Cautions about tongues

During the years of my first pastorate, I became friends with a man in the area who owned and operated two funeral homes. The relationship between our vocations commonly placed us together. He often heard me preach, pray, and even sing. On those occasions when my automobile happened to be the lead car in a funeral procession, this man would usually ride with me to the place of interment. We enjoyed each other's company, and our conversation most often centered around spiritual matters. One afternoon as we rode together, he shocked me by saying, "You've got everything you need as a preacher except one. You need to speak in tongues. When you receive that gift, you may well become one of the most powerful communicators of the gospel that anyone might desire to hear."

If he is right, then I have yet to become a powerful communicator of the gospel because I have yet to speak in tongues. If he is right, I may never become a powerful communicator of the gospel.

Through the decades of the last century, Christians have been divided by many issues, but no issue has divided Christians more deeply than the issue of tongues. On one side stands the *neocharismatic* [1] who views the second chapter of Acts as the signature chapter of authentic spiritual experience. On the other side stands the so-called noncharismatic who is so mystified and afraid of what the second chapter of Acts teaches that he or she convulses at the idea of simply trying to understand it, much less relate its truth to their own lives. The result is two-fold.

First, the neocharismatic Christian tends to claim more for the operation of the Holy Spirit than the Bible claims, which often leads to spiritual arrogance and raw emotionalism. Second, the noncharismatic Christian often fails to appropriate the power and strength of the Holy Spirit in any measure whatsoever, which can lead to dead intellectualism and dull devotion.

With Acts 2:1-4 as our foundation, we have been examining the role of the Holy Spirit in the life of the believer. In doing so, we have already spent thirteen chapters gleaning from the first three verses everything we can about the character and nature of the Spirit whom God has poured into our lives. So far, we have encountered little that is controversial. That is about to change. Acts 2:4 says: "They were all filled with the Holy Spirit and began to speak with other tongues, as the Spirit was giving them utterance."

I want to do three things with this verse. First, to tell you what I think verse 4 does not mean—that will be the thrust of this chapter. Second, I want to tell you in the next chapter what verse 4 meant for those who experienced this amazing phenomenon on the day of Pentecost. Third, in this book's final chapter I want to tell you what verse 4 means for those who follow Christ some twenty centuries later.

TONGUE TIED: NOT A NORMATIVE EXPERIENCE

Verse 4 is not establishing a normative experience for everyone who is filled with the Holy Spirit. That is, the experience of Acts 2:4 is not meant to be the experience of everyone who comes to know the Lord Jesus Christ personally. The particular event that occurred in this verse is not to be repeated each time the Holy Spirit takes up residence in a person's life. How do I know that? Two reasons. First, if the experience of the 120 men and women in this upper room should be considered the norm, then we would expect to see at every spiritual birth the re-enactment of Acts 2:1-4 — not merely the phenomenon of speaking in other tongues but also the sound of a violent rushing wind, and the appearance of flames resting on those who are saved. Yet only one of these three wonders occurred again in Acts, and the occurrence of that one is recorded only twice more in the remainder of the New Testament. I submit to you that if the second chapter of Acts is the norm, then we would see all these things taking place again and again. However, the fact is, we do not—even in Scripture.

Let me give you another example. In verses 14-36 of Acts 2, Peter preaches the first sermon of the newly born church. Three thousand people repented and were baptized:

> Now when they heard this, they were pierced to the heart, and said to Peter and the rest of the apostles, "Brethren, what shall we do?" And Peter said to them, "Repent, and let each of you be baptized in the name

of Jesus Christ for the forgiveness of your sins; and you shall receive the gift of the Holy Spirit. For the promise is for you and your children and for all who are far off, as many as the Lord our God shall call to Himself." ... So then, those who had received his word were baptized; and there were added that day about three thousand souls. (Acts 2: 37-41)

According to these verses, the Holy Spirit fell upon 3,000 men and women. Did a noise like a violent, rushing wind sound forth again? Did flames of fire rest upon any of the 3,000 as they did upon the 120? Did this vast throng of new disciples speak in tongues? If any one of the three phenomena occurred in verses 37-41, there is absolutely no record of it. I don't know about you, but I am hard-pressed to believe that Luke would say nothing about 3,000 people speaking in tongues. Not one marvel occurring in the early verses of Acts 2 is recorded as occurring in the latter verses. Any argument to the contrary is an argument from silence.

TONGUE TIED: NOT THE TRUE TEST OF SPIRITUALITY

The second reason that I believe Acts 2:1-4 is not the normative experience for those who receive the Holy Spirit is contained in 1 Corinthians 12:29-30: "All are not apostles, are they? All are not prophets, are they? All are not teachers, are they? All are not workers of miracles, are they? All do not have gifts of healings, do they? All do not speak with tongues, do they? All do not interpret, do they?" The grammatical construction of Paul's questions demands a negative answer — of course not!

Suppose I said, "All professional baseball players, if they are real athletes, play third base." You would think I had lost my mind. Suppose I said, "All musicians, if they are real musicians, play the saxophone." You would call me crazy. Suppose I said,

"All educators, if they are real educators, teach science." You would be highly offended, especially if you teach English or French. Is it any different if someone comes along and says, "All Christians, if they are truly spiritual, speak in tongues?" Of course not. Regardless of what you believe about tongues, Paul is clear that all Christians do not speak in tongues; that is, tongues are not the norm. To expect all Christians to speak in tongues is a tremendous miscalculation.

Some might respond by saying, "Well, all Christians may not speak in tongues, but the most spiritual Christians certainly do."

I couldn't disagree more. Notice what Paul writes in the last phrase of 1 Corinthians 12:3: "No one can say, 'Jesus is Lord,' except by the Holy Spirit." Anyone who has placed himself or herself under the Lordship of Jesus Christ is a spiritual person, a deeply spiritual person. The true test of spirituality is not the manifestation of tongues or any other supernatural ability. The true test of spirituality is the centrality of Jesus in the life.

Verse 3 does not refer to the mere verbal affirmation of Lordship. Jesus said in Matthew 7:21, "Not everyone who says to me, 'Lord, Lord,' will enter the kingdom of heaven." Lordship means servanthood. Lordship means total devotion. Lordship means to be under the sovereignty and control of the one who is Lord. If at any point in your past you genuinely surrendered the throne of your heart and life to Jesus, you were—in that moment—fully embraced and empowered by the Holy Spirit! Not only that, if you walk into a worship center today or tomorrow still surrendered to the Lordship of Jesus Christ, then you continue to be fully embraced and empowered by the Spirit—whether you have ever spoken in tongues or ever will.

TONGUE TIED: NOT A PRAYER LANGUAGE

Acts 2:4 is not establishing a normative experience for everyone who is born-again or who is filled with the Holy Spirit.

Neither does Acts 2:4 introduce us to an ecstatic, unintelligible prayer language. There are those who say that it does, but they are in error. Look at verses 5-12:

> There were Jews living in Jerusalem, devout men from every nation under heaven. And when this sound occurred, the crowd came together, and were bewildered because each one of them was hearing them speak in his own language. And they were amazed and astonished, saying, "Why, are not all these who are speaking Galileans? And how is it that we each hear them in our own language to which we were born? ... we hear them in our own tongues speaking of the mighty deeds of God." And they all continued in amazement and great perplexity, saying to one another, "What does this mean?"

Nowhere in these verses, especially verse 6 ("Each one of them was hearing them speak in his own language"), verse 8 ("We each hear them in our own language to which we were born") and verse 11 ("We hear them in our own tongue"), does Luke give us any indication that the tongues of Acts 2 are related to some ecstatic, unknown language of the angels. Instead, we are clearly told that this particular manifestation of the Spirit is that of a foreign language never studied by the speaker.

Let's suppose that the Holy Spirit fell upon you right now in the precise manner that He fell upon the men and women in the second chapter of Acts. You would not be speaking in some unknown heavenly language. You would be speaking in Russian, or Italian, or Chinese, or French, or some other language belonging to the multitudinous tribes of the global village. If it happened to you as it happened in Acts 2, you would suddenly be given the ability to communicate in a human language or tongue that you had never studied or learned.

SPEAKING OUT ABOUT TONGUES: CONCLUSIONS

Conclusion 1: Not for All Christians

You can be filled with the Holy Spirit and never speak in tongues. Only three times in Scripture is speaking in tongues directly associated with the filling of the Spirit. However, the Scripture records dozens of occasions when people were filled with the Spirit apart from any association with tongues.

Think also about this: Jesus never spoke in tongues. If He did, the biblical record is silent about any such occurrence. Further, Jesus never promised or hinted that any of His followers would speak in some ecstatic, unintelligible prayer language. In fact, He never—not once—raised the issue. Yet He emphatically promised His followers that they would be fully embraced by the Holy Spirit. "He who believes in Me, as the Scripture said, 'From His innermost being shall flow rivers of living water.' But this He spoke of the Holy Spirit, whom those who believed in Him were to receive" (John 7:38-39). Jesus promised His followers that the presence of the Holy Spirit would be like rivers of water flowing into their lives. The Holy Spirit would come upon those who trusted Him as torrents of rain, that is, they would be deluged by the power and presence of the Holy Spirit.

Conclusion 2: No Tongues Isn't Second Class

Don't let anyone relegate you to second-class status as a Christian because you do not speak in tongues. Did the 3,000 men and women at the end of Acts 2 have any less of the Spirit than the 120 men and women who had been present in that upper room? Were the 3,000 any less filled than the 120? If so, Luke fails to make such a distinction. Though the latter group did not speak in tongues, Luke leaves no doubt that the 3,000 had received the Holy Spirit. How do I know that? Because of Peter's words in verses 38-39: "Repent, ... and you shall receive the gift of the Holy Spirit. For the promise is for you and your children and for all who are far off, as many as the Lord our God shall call to Himself."

Has the Lord called you to Himself? Have you responded to His call by means of repentance? Has your focus been changed from the self-way of approaching life to the Jesus-way of approaching life? Then, according to the Word of God and the promise of Jesus, you have received the Holy Spirit—so much so that you have as much of the Spirit as any other Christian could hope to have. Take confidence in another promise of Christ concerning the Spirit: "If you ... being evil, know how to give good gifts to your children, how much more will your heavenly Father give the Holy Spirit to those who ask Him?" (Luke 11:13)

Conclusion 3: Judge by Scripture

Judge your experience by Scripture rather than judging Scripture by your experience. Experience can be false; Scripture cannot. I once served on a church staff with a woman who became involved in the neocharismatic movement. Unfortunately, her experience meant more to her than scriptural revelation. She began to base her theology upon what she experienced rather than on Scripture itself. Her thinking was something like this: "I have had this experience; therefore, the Bible must mean this." However, Scripture is to be the final judge and arbiter of any experience we might have.

NOTES

[1] By *modern-day charismatic* or *neocharismatic*, I am referring to those who believe that the spiritual gifts of the early church, without exception, are still in operation today. I view myself as a charismatic; that is, I believe wholeheartedly in the gifts, ministries, and energies of the Holy Spirit. Further, I want the congregations I serve to be charismatic congregations; that is, I want my people to discover their individual gifts, to know the specific ministries in which those gifts are to be utilized, and to operate under the full anointing of the Holy Spirit. At the same time, I believe that some of the gifts and ministries available in the historical era of the New Testament are unavailable today. That belief has nothing to do with a lack of faith on my part, but has resulted from what I consider to be serious theological and biblical study. When the purpose for certain gifts and ministries passed, then the gift passed from the scene as well. For a deeper examination of spiritual gifts, ministries and energies, see my book, *Divine Designs: The Power of Knowing Who You Are and What You Do Best* .

The Holy Spirit Workout #14

THINKING ABOUT TONGUES

It's important for all Christians to understand the controversy over tongues because it goes to the heart of Spiritual gifts and their ability to empower our lives. What are your answers to these questions?

1. Why has the manifestation of tongues been so divisive in the realm of Christianity?
2. Based on Acts 2, is speaking in tongues to be seen as a heavenly prayer language?
3. Is speaking in tongues the norm for men and women who are filled with the Spirit? Why or why not?
4. According to 1 Corinthians 12, do all Christians speak in tongues?
5. For you, what is the true test of spirituality?
6. If Pentecost occurred in your church today, what languages might the congregation be speaking?
7. Did Jesus speak in tongues?
8. What promise concerning the Spirit did Jesus make to all who would follow Him?
9. If the Spirit has been manifested in your life in a fashion similar to that of Acts 2, is there a particular vocation for which you might be well suited?
10. How can you be a peacemaker in regard to this divisive issue?

Paul reveals the purpose for tongues: To serve as a "sign" to unbelievers. Two questions are in order. Who are these unbelievers? What do they not believe?

Chapter Fifteen

Tongues: A Sign of the Times

They ... began to speak with other tongues ....
"What does this mean?"
– Acts 2:4, 12

In this chapter you will learn:

* How the Holy Spirit equipped the early believers
* Irrefutable evidence that God wanted to give the Holy Spirit to Gentiles as well as Jews
* Four things that tongues tell us about God
* A glorious truth about the goodness of Christ

In the last chapter we discovered what Acts 2:4 does not mean. It does not establish a normative experience for all who follow Christ or for all who are filled with the Holy Spirit, nor does Acts 2:4 introduce us to an ecstatic, unintelligible prayer language. So, what did Acts 2:4 mean to those who were present on the day of Pentecost? Only by answering that can Acts 2:4 have meaning for the Christian today.

EQUIPPING HIS WITNESSES

The ability to speak in foreign languages never studied can be seen as a direct fulfillment of the promise made by Jesus in Acts 1:8: "You will receive power when the Holy Spirit has come upon you; and you shall be My witness both in Jerusalem, and in all Judea and Samaria, and even to the remotest part of the earth." You and I may use Acts 1:8 as a plan for our ever-widening circle of mission responsibility. For me and my present congregation, we begin in Savannah; then we go to Georgia; then we go to America; then we go to the world—even the deserts and jungles—anywhere people happen to be. This verse, coupled with Matthew 28:19-20, is the driving force behind the mission efforts of most denominations and churches. This verse guides us in most every endeavor and decision.

Like us, there is no doubt that Peter and his friends considered Acts 1:8 to be their manifesto. Yet, for Peter and his friends, Acts 1:8 was much more. Acts 1:8 would be fulfilled by them—both literally and personally. You and I may be part of an organization that starts at home with all of its people and goes to other parts of the world with some of its people. However, Peter and those who stood with him in Acts 2 would not just send others—they would go themselves. In Acts 2, at the birth of the church, there would be no time for language school. Many of the people in that upper room would go immediately to various parts of the world proclaiming the Kingdom of God. What we see in Acts 2:4 is nothing more than the Holy Spirit equipping these early believers for the task that stood directly before them. There could be no excuses—God had given them everything they needed to follow His directive.

TO GENTILES AND JEWS

The ability to speak in foreign languages never studied was irrefutable evidence that God wanted to give the Holy Spirit to

Gentiles as well as to Jews. Look at 1 Corinthians 14:22: "Tongues are for a sign, not to those who believe but to unbelievers." In this verse Paul gives us the purpose for tongues: They are to serve as a sign to unbelievers; that is, God will use this particular manifestation of the Spirit as a way to deliver a message or to give evidence of His kingdom to those who do not believe.

Two questions are in order here. First, who are these unbelievers? The unbelievers are Jews.[1] In particular, they are Jews who had accepted Christ as the promised Messiah. How do I know that? I'll show you in a moment. The second question is what did these Jewish Christians not believe? They did not believe that God would save non-Jews. They taught that if a person wanted to be saved, the person had to become a Jew first. This person not only had to be circumcised (if this person happened to be a man), but he or she had to ascribe also to the laws of Judaism as given by Moses.

Of course, these Jewish Christians were wrong, but that is what they believed. This issue of who could be saved and who could not be saved didn't arise in Acts 2 because the entire crowd was Jewish. Many of those who were present that day had traveled from far away places to be in Jerusalem for the festival of Pentecost; nonetheless, they were Jews. You may be amazed to know that in spite of what happened in Acts 2, five years passed before these Jewish Christians began to see or acknowledge their responsibility to take the gospel to non-Jews. Here is what turned these Jewish Christians around. Acts 10:1-48 says:

> Now there was a man at Caesarea named Cornelius, a centurion of what was called the Italian cohort, a devout man and one who feared God with all his household, and gave many alms to the Jewish people and prayed to God continually. About the ninth hour of the day he clearly saw in a vision an angel of God

who had just come in and said to him, "Cornelius!" And fixing his gaze on him and being much alarmed, he said, "What is it, Lord?" And he said to him, "Your prayers and alms have ascended as a memorial before God. Now dispatch some men to Joppa and send for a man named Simon, who is also called Peter; he is staying with a tanner named Simon, whose house is by the sea." When the angel who was speaking to him had left, he summoned two of his servants and a devout soldier of those who were his personal attendants, and after he had explained everything to them, he sent them to Joppa.

On the next day, as they were on their way and approaching the city, Peter went up on the housetop about the sixth hour to pray. But he became hungry and was desiring to eat; but while they were making preparations, he fell into a trance; and he saw the sky opened up, and an object like a great sheet coming down, lowered by four corners to the ground, and there were in it all kinds of four-footed animals and crawling creatures of the earth and birds of the air. And a voice came to him, "Get up, Peter, kill and eat!" But Peter said, "By no means, Lord, for I have never eaten anything unholy and unclean." Again a voice came to him a second time, "What God has cleansed, no longer consider unholy." And this happened three times; and immediately the object was taken up into the sky.

Now while Peter was greatly perplexed in mind as to what the vision which he had seen might be, behold, the men who had been sent by Cornelius, having asked directions for Simon's house, appeared at the gate; and calling out, they were asking whether

Simon, who was also called Peter, was staying there. While Peter was reflecting on the vision, the Spirit said to him, "Behold, three men are looking for you. But get up, go downstairs and accompany them without misgivings, for I have sent them Myself." Peter went down to the men and said, "Behold, I am the one you are looking for; what is the reason for which you have come?" They said, "Cornelius, a centurion, a right-eous and God-fearing man well spoken of by the entire nation of the Jews, was divinely directed by a holy angel to send for you to come to his house and hear a message from you." So he invited them in and gave them lodging.

And on the next day he got up and went away with them, and some of the brethren from Joppa accompa-nied him. On the following day he entered Caesarea. Now Cornelius was waiting for them and had called together his relatives and close friends. When Peter entered, Cornelius met him, and fell at his feet and wor-shiped him. But Peter raised him up, saying, "Stand up; I too am a just a man." As he talked with him, he entered and found many people assembled. And he said to them, "You yourselves know how unlawful it is for a man who is a Jew to associate with a foreigner or to visit him; and yet God has shown me that I should not call any man unholy or unclean. That is why I came with-out even raising any objection when I was sent for. So I ask for what reason you have sent for me."

Cornelius said, "Four days ago to this hour, I was praying in my house during the ninth hour; and behold, a man stood before me in shining garments, and he said, 'Cornelius, your prayer has been heard and your alms have been remembered before God.

Therefore send to Joppa and invite Simon, who is also called Peter, to come to you; he is staying at the house of Simon the tanner by the sea.' So I sent for you immediately, and you have been kind enough to come. Now then, we are all here present before God to hear all that you have been commanded by the Lord."

Opening his mouth, Peter said: "I most certainly understand now that God is not one to show partiality, but in every nation the man who fears Him and does what is right is welcome to Him. The word which He sent to the sons of Israel, preaching peace through Jesus Christ (He is Lord of all)—you yourselves know the thing which took place throughout all Judea, starting from Galilee, after the baptism which John proclaimed. You know of Jesus of Nazareth, how God anointed Him with the Holy Spirit and with power, and how He went about doing good and healing all who were oppressed by the devil; for God was with Him. We are witnesses of all the things He did both in the land of the Jews and in Jerusalem. They also put Him to death by hanging Him on a cross. God raised Him up on the third day and granted that He should become visible, not to all the people, but to witnesses who were chosen beforehand by God, that is, to us, who ate and drank with Him after He arose from the dead. And He ordered us to preach to the people, and solemnly to testify that this is the One who has been appointed by God as Judge of the living and the dead. Of Him all the prophets bear witness that through His name everyone who believes in Him receives forgiveness of sins."

While Peter was still speaking these words, the Holy Spirit fell upon all those who were listening to the message. All the circumcised believers who had come with Peter were amazed, because the gift of the Holy Spirit had been poured out on the Gentiles also. For they were hearing them speaking with tongues and exalting God. Then Peter answered, "Surely no one can refuse the water for these to be baptized who have received the Holy Spirit just as we did, can he?" And he ordered them to be baptized in the name of Jesus Christ.

GOD'S OPEN-DOOR POLICY

In Acts 10, the Jewish Christians who accompanied Peter to Joppa came to realize that God meant for the door of faith to be open to the Gentiles (non-Jews) just as that door had been opened to the Jews. For the first time, Peter and his Jewish friends began to understand that "God is not one to show partiality, but in every nation the man who fears Him and does what is right is welcome to Him" (Acts 10: 34-35). As Peter preached the gospel to Cornelius and the other Gentiles in his home, the Holy Spirit fell upon all those who were listening. By the way, Cornelius was not only a Gentile, he was also a Roman soldier. That fact made him the worst of the worst—at least as far as most Jews were concerned. Those Jews who witnessed this marvelous event with Peter were amazed at what they observed. They were astounded that God would accept the Gentiles into His kingdom without those Gentiles first becoming Jews.

How did Peter and his Jewish associates know that God was willing to grant salvation to the Gentiles and shower them with the Holy Spirit? Verses 46-47 provide the answer: "For they were hearing them speaking with tongues and exalting God. Then Peter answered, 'Surely no one can refuse the water for these to be baptized who have received the Holy Spirit just as we did, can he?'" Note the phrase in verse 47, *just as we did*. Cornelius and his Gentile associates had the same experience of speaking in foreign languages never studied as the 120 did on the Day of Pentecost. Thus, in accordance with 1 Corinthians 14:22, tongues served as a sign to Jewish Christians who did not believe that God would pour out His Spirit upon the Gentiles without first becoming Jews.

In Acts 15, Peter recounted this event to those present at the Jerusalem Council as irrefutable evidence that the Gentiles did not have to become Jews before God would accept them. Again, many Jewish Christians—especially those who had come from the sect of the Pharisees—kept insisting that the Gentiles be circumcised and instructed to follow the Law of Moses as conditions for salvation (*see* Acts 14:26-15:6). However, Peter put the matter to rest in verses 7-10 of Acts 15:

> Peter stood up and said to them, "Brethren, you know that in the early days God made a choice among you, that by my mouth the Gentiles would hear the word of the gospel and believe. And God, who knows the heart, bore witness to them, giving them the Holy Spirit, just as He also did to us; and He made no distinction between us and them, cleansing their hearts by faith. Now therefore why do you put God to the test by placing upon the neck of the disciples a yoke which neither our fathers nor we have been able to bear?"

Had God not blessed the early church with the gift of tongues, Christianity may well have remained a radical splinter group within the framework of Judaism. The manifestation of tongues—foreign languages never studied—paved the way for Jews and Gentiles to come together as one body in the life and work of the church. Indeed, tongues were given as a sign of the times and for the times.

George W. Zeller has written some noteworthy comments concerning this purpose of tongues:

> Tongues point to the fact that God was doing something new and different! No longer would God's witness be a nation ... but God's witness would be among all nations ... No longer would Jerusalem be the focal point ... rather it would be merely the starting point ... No longer would God's message go only to the lost sheep of the house of Israel ... but it would go to every nation and kindred and people and tongue ...
>
> It is highly significant that on this special day [Pentecost in Acts 2] God had Jewish representatives present from every nation under heaven. It is as if God were saying to these Jews: I want you to understand what is involved in My "new program," and I want you to appreciate the worldwide scope of My great commission ... I am going to give you an audio-visual aid (namely, "tongues") to show you that God's message is going to go to every nation under Heaven... .[2]

A GOD WITHOUT LIMITS: FOUR CONCLUSIONS ABOUT TONGUES

God Is Not Limited by Love

The Jews said, "God loves only us." However, the manifestation of tongues clearly demonstrated that God's love extended to every race, every nationality, and every tribe or people group. God's love is as great and as profound for the black man and the red man and the yellow man as it is for the Jewish white man — there is no distinction. Therefore, when we make distinctions we are unmistakably in the wrong.

God Is Not Limited by Likeness

The Jews said, "You've got to be like us." However, the manifestation of tongues clearly demonstrates that God does not attempt to make carbon copies of those who follow Him. We are all different, and our uniqueness is a deliberate part of God's creative design. Your hair doesn't have to be like mine. Your clothes don't have to be like mine. Your methodology doesn't have to be like mine. Your worship style doesn't have to be like mine. You can be unlike me in many ways and still be a serious follower of Jesus Christ. We have no right to insist that others be spiritual clones of ourselves.

God Is Not Limited by Location

The Jews said, "God is at work only in Jerusalem." However, the manifestation of tongues clearly demonstrated that God is not only working *here*, He is also working *there*. God is not only at work in your church or in your denomination or in your organization; He is at work in other churches and in other denominations and other organizations. Many Christians grow quite arrogant thinking that God is more at home with us than with anyone else. John once said to Jesus, "Master, we saw someone casting out demons in Your name; and we tried to prevent him because he does not follow along with us" (Luke 9:49). In effect, John was saying, "God can't be at work in that man's life because he is not in our group!"

How did Jesus respond? "Do not hinder him; for he who is not against you is for you" (Luke 9:50).

God Is Not Limited by Legacy

The Jews said, "If you want to be saved, you've got to keep the law perfectly." The manifestation of tongues clearly told those Jews their thinking was wrong. When a person's past is decorated with failure, wrongdoing, or even degradation,

God still has a future for that person. Never forget this glorious truth—we are not saved by depending upon our goodness. Rather, we are saved by depending upon the goodness of Jesus Christ.

NOTES

[1] There are those who say that these unbelievers are non-Christians, that somehow, tongues have an evangelistic appeal or significance to those who have not yet become disciples of Christ. However, that is not likely the case. If it is, then tongues would be a sign giving evidence to the outside world that the Christian community had lost its sanity. In 1 Corinthians 14:23 Paul said, "If the whole church assembles together and all speak in tongues, and ungifted men or unbelievers enter, will they not say that you are mad?"

[2] George W. Zeller, *God's Gift of Tongues: the Nature, Purpose, and Duration of Tongues as Taught in the Bible* (Neptune, NJ: Loizeaux Brothers, 1978), pp. 27-30.

The Holy Spirit Workout #15

UNDERSTANDING THE PURPOSE OF TONGUES

Like all gifts of the Holy Spirit, the ability to speak in tongues served an important purpose in the early days of the Christian church. To better understand the role of tongues in the church today, it is important that we are clear about what Scripture relates to us about this ability. Test your knowledge of the purpose of tongues by answering the following questions.

1. What promise of Jesus was fulfilled by the manifestation of tongues, as recorded in Acts?
2. Tongues served as a sign. To whom? For what?
3. Why is the story of Cornelius, in Acts 10, so important?
4. What might the church be like today if tongues had not been manifested in Acts 2 and 10?
5. How did Peter's experience in Acts 10 prove useful in subsequent chapters of Acts?
6. What do you think George Zeller means when he describes tongues as an "audio-visual aid"?
7. What preconceived limitations of early Jewish Christians did tongues help to pull down?
8. Who does God love?
9. Where does God work?
10. How is a person made right with God?

The church at Corinth was anything but a model church. Paul spent more time admonishing this factious congregation than he did any other. This fellowship was riddled with problems. He gave approximately 20 percent of his letter attempting to correct their chaotic confusion about spiritual gifts.

Chapter Sixteen

Tongues: *for the* Twenty-First Century

Greater is one who prophesies than one who speaks in tongues.
– 1 Corinthians 14:5

In this chapter you will learn:

* If angels speak in tongues
* When the expression of tongues becomes counterfeit
* Foundational principles for a genuine spiritual gift
* Paul's six guidelines for tongues

In his book *Touching the Heart of God*, Ernest J. Gruen wrote:

> Tongues is one of the keys to the Christian life. It's the difference between going somewhere on a scooter and going somewhere in a Cadillac ... If we will worship God in tongues every day, then the Spirit will flow in us and we will be full ... If we don't pray in tongues daily, we're missing the point. The gift of praying in tongues is the supernatural means of staying Spirit-filled.[1]

If what Gruen writes is true, there are many followers of Jesus Christ who are scooter-ridin' disciples. If what Gruen wrote is true, then many of us have lived our Christian lives in vain. If what Gruen wrote is true, the members of the church I pastor are missing the point.

Of course, there are many neocharismatics who think that, indeed, we have missed the point. I learned a long time ago not to make sweeping, all-inclusive statements, and I'm not going to do that now, but there are those who think that we at Calvary in Savannah are as dead as canned tuna. They think we know nothing of deep spirituality because we do not fling ourselves into the tongues phenomenon, which they describe as speaking in ecstatic, unintelligible prayer languages that supposedly communicate with God in special ways.

CONFUSED IN CORINTH, AGAIN?

We have already examined the manifestation of tongues in the book of Acts, and we have discovered not the use of angelic or heavenly languages, but rather the ability to speak in a foreign language of the human race—a foreign language never studied or learned by the speaker. The Scripture is absolutely clear on this point. That being the case, where do neocharismatics find biblical basis for their teaching on tongues? They find it in a hugely troubled and schismatic Christian congregation known to us as the church at Corinth.

As we begin our study of 1 Corinthians 14, it's important to understand that the church at Corinth was anything but a model congregation. In fact, the apostle Paul spent more time and energy correcting and admonishing the members of this factious church than he did any other congregation under his tutelage. Even a casual perusal of his letter tells the reader that this particular church was riddled with problems. Though Paul addressed many issues in the course of his sixteen-chapter dialogue, he spent three of those chapters—approximately 20 percent of his letter—attempting to correct their chaotic confusion about spiritual gifts. The Corinthians' difficulty was not the absence of spiritual gifts in their church, but rather, the lack of understanding about the operation and employment of those spiritual gifts.

What does Paul tell them about tongues? In verse 2 of chapter 14 he says, "For one who speaks in a tongue does not speak to men, but to God; for no one understands, but in his spirit he speaks mysteries." There is no question that we encounter in this verse a reference to a language that can be described as an ecstatic, unintelligible utterance. However, what do we learn about this strange utterance? First, according to verse 2, we learn that the speaker of this language is not addressing men, but God. Second, we learn that this speaker has absolutely no idea what he may or may not be saying. Seemingly, only God understands this utterance. What does that suggest? For starters, it suggests that this utterance is not like the utterances that are displayed in the book of Acts. The tongues on display in the book of Acts were spoken to men. Further, the utterance described in 1 Corinthians 14:2 is not like the utterances we studied in Acts because the tongues we witnessed in Acts were understood in their own language by all who were present.

Most neocharismatics would agree that the manifestation of tongues in 1 Corinthians 14:2 is different than in Acts. However, they would also not hesitate to say that the difference is not negative, but positive. That is, they believe Paul is identifying the legitimate existence of a mystical language that is a kind of supernatural way to pray or to receive instruction from God. Some refer to this mystical language as an angelic utterance. I respond to such an assertion by observing that the Bible never—not once—records an angel speaking in a language other than one that was naturally understood by the listener.

Others say that this mystical language is an utterance of the

Holy Spirit Himself as He prays on our behalf. They point to Romans 8:26 which says, "The Spirit Himself intercedes for us with groanings too deep for words." Yet, does not the fact that the prayers of the Spirit are *too deep for words* eliminate the possibility that groanings become words? Surely, the Holy Spirit performs His intercession in the very presence of God as does Jesus Himself. Further, when the Spirit is standing on my behalf before God, why would He need my mouth or vocal cords?

I once stood at the bedside of a woman who was dying. She couldn't speak, but she could groan. As she attempted to communicate with me, someone brought a writing pad and a pencil to the bedside, but this woman couldn't write. Then a letter board was brought, but this woman didn't have the stability in her hands to form the words. However, as she looked in my eyes and desperately tried to tell me something, it suddenly dawned on me what she wanted. As I spoke, she became quiet and shook her head in the affirmative. No words. No syllables. Just groanings. God understands the groanings of the Spirit without words of any kind. And why shouldn't He? God and the Spirit are One.

A TONGUE LASHING, PART ONE

Let's also consider some interesting grammatical possibilities in 1 Corinthians 14:2: "For one who speaks in a tongue does not speak to men, but to God; for no one understands, but in his spirit he speaks mysteries." The word translated *God* is the Greek word *theo*, and it appears in the Greek manuscript without the use of the definite article. That means we could translate this particular word as lower case rather than upper case: "One who speaks in a tongue does not speak to men, but to 'a god.'" In other words, the person speaking this mysterious language is addressing a pagan god rather than the One True God. Now look at the word translated *spirit*, appropriately rendered as a lower case noun in most translations. Again, the grammatical construction here easily supports the idea of a pagan god as the driving force behind this mysterious language so that the last phrase of verse 2 could be translated: "but by means of the spirit of this pagan god he speaks mysteries." If that translation is correct, then Paul is revealing a counterfeit expression of the genuine gift of tongues—a fraudulent manifestation planted by the forces of darkness to bring confusion, pride, and turmoil to the Corinthian church.

In fact, there are Greek scholars who say that each time Paul uses the singular word *tongue*, he is referring to the counterfeit expression of this gift; and when he uses the plural word *tongues* (as employed in the book of Acts and in the list of spiritual gifts found in 1 Corinthians 12:8-10) he has in mind the genuine gift. According to this view, Paul simply moves back and forth between the true ability (*tongues*) and the fraudulent ability (*tongue*).

There are those who use verse 4, "One who speaks in a tongue edifies himself," to say that Paul is revealing a kind of tongue that is for devotional, private use—a mysterious language that enriches and refreshes the inner man. However, I believe verse 4 is not meant to be taken in a positive light but in a negative light. Why? Because this particular manifestation, whatever it is, violates one of the foundational principles of a genuine spiritual gift: the advancement of the church. First Corinthians 12:7 says, "To each one is given the manifestation of the Spirit for the common good." Clearly, spiritual gifts are not distributed by God for private use, but for the good of the church at large. My spiritual capacities are not to be spent on me, but on you. My spiritual abilities are not to point to me, but to God! Notice the last three words of 1 Corinthians 14:4, "edifies the church." Look at the last phrase of 1 Corinthians 14:5, "that the church may receive edifying." Look at the second half of 1 Corinthians 14:12, "seek to abound for the edification of the church." Go to the last phrase of 1 Corinthians 14:26, "Let all things be done for edification;" that is, the edification of the church.

When Paul says in verse 4, "One who speaks in a tongue edifies himself," he is not being kind. To the contrary, he is depicting the use of this mysterious language as a kind of selfish, attention-getting ploy to enhance one's reputation as a spiritual giant or master. Some of the folks at Corinth were saying, "Hey, gang, look at me! Look at what I'm doing! Wow, am I spiritual! You need to do this and you'll be spiritual too!" When verse 4 is placed in context with Paul's broader teaching on spiritual gifts, he could not be more clear that the overwhelming purpose of spiritual gifts is not that of self-edification, but that of lifting up and encouraging fellow members of the church at large.

A TONGUE LASHING, PART TWO

Here is what I think was happening in the Corinthian church. Many of these people had been deeply involved in the pagan temples that characterized the Greek culture in which they lived. Scholars and historians tell us that one of the ritual practices within these temples was chanting, that is, speaking in an unintelligible gibberish to the pagan gods whom the temples were built to honor. Apparently, this particular experience not only had great power over the participants but great appeal as well. Of course, those who could perform these chants were recognized as masters of their cultic religion. When these people came to know Christ and joined the Corinthian church, they brought this pagan practice with them. The thinking was: "That which made me a master among the cults will now make me a master among the Christians." The result was rank confusion and constant argument.

Paul could have confronted this issue head-on, but to do so would have resulted in even greater confusion. Why? Because most people give more weight to personal experience than they do to truth. If Paul had started out by saying, "You're experience is false," he would have lost his audience immediately. They would have said, "I hear you Paul, but I know what my experience has been. You simply do not understand." Consequently, Paul comes in from the side door—so to speak—and tells them how genuine spiritual gifts operate.

Good parents frequently take this nonconfrontational, off-angle approach. For example, suppose you had a sixteen-year-old daughter who came to you and said, "I'm in love. I've finally found Mr. Right. I know who I want to spend the rest of my life with." If you responded by saying, "Ha! You have no idea what love is. You're in love with love. This is not real—it's nothing more than puppy love," three things would likely happen. First, you would make her angry. Second, you would forfeit any opportunity for effective communication with her on this topic for a long time into the future. Third, you would make her more steadfast in her view. However, if you responded with creative affirmations, you would leave the door open to numerous conversations about the genuine manifestation of love, and ultimately she would come around to your way of thinking. Now, which way is the wisest way to respond, the first or the second? The second way, of course. Why? Because this sixteen-year-old girl is immature and her love is immature.

Did you know that Paul wrote to a group of Christians whom he likened to milk-drinking babies? Look at 1 Corinthians 3:1-3, "I, brethren, could not speak to you as to spiritual men, but as to men of flesh, as to infants in Christ. I gave you milk to drink, not solid food; for you were not yet able to receive it. Indeed, even now you are not yet able, for you are still fleshly ... and ... are you not walking like mere men?"

Now look at 1 Corinthians 14:20, "Do not be children in your thinking ... but in your thinking be mature." Paul is facing an audience that is spiritually immature, so he writes in a way they can understand. Rather than criticize their personal experience—which would likely result in more harm than help at this point—he attempts to guide their personal experience until they are able to think more maturely.

STRAIGHT TALK ABOUT TONGUES

Beginning with I Corinthians 14:5, Paul presented three general guidelines concerning tongues. The first guideline is found in verses 5-12:

> I wish that you all spoke in tongues, but even more that you would prophesy; and greater is one who prophesies than one who speaks in tongues, unless he interprets, so that the church may receive edifying. But now, brethren, if I come to you speaking in tongues, what will I profit you unless I speak to you either by way of revelation or of knowledge or of prophecy or of teaching? Yet even lifeless things, either flute or harp, in producing a sound, if they do not produce a distinction in the tones, how will it be known what is played on the flute or on the harp? For if the bugle produces an indistinct sound, who will prepare himself for battle? So also you, unless you utter by the tongue speech that is clear, how will it be known what is spoken? For you will be speaking into the air. There are, perhaps, a great many kinds of languages in the world, and no kind is without meaning. If then I do not know the meaning of the language, I will be to the one who speaks a barbarian, and the one who speaks will be a barbarian to me. So also you, since you are zealous of spiritual gifts, seek to abound for the edification of the church.

Paul's guideline is that any time you are communicating on

behalf of God, your communication should be as easy to understand as it is relevant to the lives of the listeners. The greatest thing you can do for another person is to show him or her how the Word of God intersects with the everyday experience of life. Make the Word address their particular need, and do so in a way they can readily comprehend. Paul is saying, "If you insist on speaking in these mystical languages, then make sure that you or someone else can interpret exactly what you are saying. If an interpreter is not present, then you have no business saying anything at all. Otherwise, you sound like a barbarian and you might as well be speaking into the air."

The second guideline is found in verses 13-17:

> Let one who speaks in a tongue pray that he may interpret. For if I pray in a tongue, my spirit prays, but my mind is unfruitful. What is the outcome then? I will pray with the spirit and I will pray with the mind also; I will sing with the spirit and I will sing with the mind also. Otherwise if you bless in the spirit only, how will the one who fills the place of the ungifted say the "Amen" at your giving of thanks, since he does not know what you are saying? For you are giving thanks well enough, but the other person is not edified.

Paul's second guideline is to keep your mind and your tongue engaged at all times. Paul did not say that he prayed in a tongue, but rather, he said, "*If* I pray in a tongue." The grammatical construction of this phrase tells us that Paul is speaking hypothetically. Paul is saying, "Suppose I were to pray in some mystical language. Then, I want to know what I'm saying. Suppose I were to sing in some mystical language. Then, I want to know what I'm singing." Why? Because this gift or ability, if it is a real gift or ability, is meant to be used to encourage others. Every gift of the Spirit, if it is a genuine gift, must satisfactorily answer the following question: How is this gift being used to strengthen and empower and encourage others? Should you practice speaking in some mystical language if you don't know what you are saying? If nobody else knows what you are saying, how useful is your ability?

The third guideline is found in verses 18-26:

> I thank God, I speak in tongues more than you all; however, in the church I desire to speak five words with my mind so that I may instruct others also, rather than ten thousand words in a tongue ... Therefore if the whole church assembles together and all speak in tongues, and ungifted men or unbelievers enter, will they not say that you are mad? But if all prophesy, and an unbeliever or an ungifted man enters, he is convicted by all, he is called into account by all; the secrets of his heart are disclosed; and so he will fall on his face and worship God, declaring that God is certainly among you. What is the outcome then, brethren? When you assemble, each one has a psalm, has a teaching, has a revelation, has a tongue, has an interpretation. Let all things be done for edification.

Paul's third guideline is that the worship experience of the church must remain on a seeker-oriented level and therefore be conducted in the language of the common man. Moreover, the ministry of the church must be done in such a way that even those who have not yet come to faith in Christ can understand. Paul says, "Look, I know all about speaking in tongues. Been there; done that. I communicate in tongues all the time." Of course, Paul is talking about the genuine article here. He is referring to the ability to speak in foreign languages never studied—as we saw utilized in the book of Acts. He is talking about the literal fulfillment of taking the gospel to the entire world, as promised by Jesus in Acts 1:8. Paul utilized this ability extensively on the mission field, especially in the presence of Jewish Christians who viewed God and salvation in a narrow, limited way—and that is his reference in verses 21-22. However, when Paul entered a local church and addressed the membership, he spoke in such a way that all could understand, even those who had little or no spiritual insight.

Despite Paul's guidelines, there were still those in Corinth who insisted on interjecting the use of some mysterious, unintelligible tongue in the worship experience of the church. In that case, Paul laid down three rules in verses 27-28, "If anyone speaks in a tongue, it should be by two or at the most three, and each in turn, and one must interpret; but if there is no interpreter, he must keep silent in the church; and let him speak to himself and to God."

- Rule #1—never more than three tongues speakers in one service.
- Rule #2—never more than one tongues speaker at a time.
- Rule #3—never a tongue speaker without an interpreter.

TONGUES: SIX WAYS TO PEACE

As we bring this study of tongues to a close, I want to draw six conclusions. The first three are for those who affirm the teaching they've read in these chapters on tongues. The second three are for those neocharismatics who are militant in their belief that no one can be a Spirit-filled Christian unless he or she speaks in some ecstatic, unintelligble utterance.

- Never attempt to refute someone who has supposedly experienced the manifestation of speaking in a mysterious spiritual language. Paul didn't try. If you try, you'll find yourself in an exercise of futility, and your efforts will only produce more argument and greater division. Simply agree to disagree in as loving a manner as possible, and go your own way.

- Stand firm on the clear teaching of Scripture that living and operating in the fullness of the Holy Spirit does not require practicing or speaking in some mysterious tongue. Allow no one to shut you out. Allow no one to relegate you to secondary status as an effective believer because you do not speak in ecstatic, unintelligible utterances. Never accept man-made criteria of spiritual anointing. Someone once told me that when the members of my congregation got filled with the Spirit, they would be jumping over pews! I thought to myself, "And where does the Bible say that?" Worship style or preference is not to be confused with the filling of the Spirit. If someone wants to roll in the aisle, raise their hands, or dance, that's fine. But don't allow anyone to make their manner of celebration a measure of the Spirit's filling in your life.

- Keep speaking the Word of God clearly and with relevance. As a result, you will see the lives of many drastically changed.

- Acknowledge and accept Paul's teaching that the disciple of Jesus Christ does not have to ask God for any particular gift, but that God gives to each of us the gifts He desires us to have. God chooses my gifts according to His pleasure, and when He gives a gift, that gift is the best I can possibly receive and that gift will be used under His anointing: "One and the same Spirit works all these things, distributing to each one individually just as He wills ...God has placed the members, each one of them, in the body, just as He desired" (1 Cor. 12:11, 18).

- If you are going to practice this mysterious language, then operate by Paul's rules publicly. Not uncommonly, neocharismatic worship lapses into a tongues free-for-all. When that happens, the Holy Spirit is playing no part. Ask yourself if you are really being spiritual in using this mysterious ability if you aren't willing to abide by the rules laid down by Paul.

- If you think you are spiritually superior because you speak in some kind of mysterious, incomprehensible language, please consider how elitism can be as unbecoming as it is divisive. Make room for other serious-minded Christians to serve God with joy, even though they view the manifestation of tongues differently.

If there are tongues, they will cease...
Now faith, hope, love, abide these three;
but the greatest of these is love.
– 1 Corinthians 13:8, 13

NOTES

[1] Ernest J. Gruen, Touching the Heart of God (Springdale, PA: Whitaker House, 1986), 172, 177.

Holy Spirit Workout #16

CONTEMPLATING TONGUES

One of the over-arching messages of *Halos of Fire* is that the Bible, the inspired word of God, supplies us the truth we need to make decisions about our life and our faith. This final chapter has focused on some historical truths about tongues. Answer the following questions to determine how the facts and conclusions presented affect your view of tongues.

1. Where do neocharismatic Christians find biblical support for their view that tongues is a kind of heavenly prayer language?
2. How does their view conflict with Paul's clear principles of spiritual gifts?
3. Does the Bible ever give examples of angels speaking in languages other than those spoken by the listener?
4. Did Jesus ever speak in tongues or encourage His followers to do so?
5. What possible connection did the pagan religions of Corinth have to the tongues phenomenon Paul addressed?
6. Did the church at Corinth display maturity as a Christian congregation?
7. Is the Corinthian church better used as a how-to model or a how-not-to model?
8. What guidelines did Paul lay down regarding the use of tongues in worship?9. Can a Christian be deeply spiritual and not practice the neocharismatic view of tongues?

Someone once said that the future is as bright as the promises of God. If that is true, then your future is exploding with light.

Chapter Seventeen

Final Thoughts

CONSIDER THE PROMISES OF GOD CONCERNING THE HOLY SPIRIT.

1. The Spirit inhabits the body of every believer.
   - "Repent ... and you will receive the gift of the Holy Spirit. This promise is for you" (Acts 2:38).
   - "Do you not know that your body is a temple of the Holy Spirit who is in you?" (1Cor. 6:19)

2. The Spirit empowers us as witnesses for the kingdom of God.
   - You will receive power when the Holy Spirit has come upon you; and you shall be My witnesses" (Acts 1:8).
   - With great power (they) were giving testimony to

the resurrection of the Lord Jesus, and abundant grace was upon them all" (Acts 4:33).

3. The Spirit equips us for divinely designed service.
    - "To each one is given the manifestation of the Spirit for the common good" (1 Cor. 12:7)
    - "The ... Spirit works all these things, distributing to each one individually just as He wills" (1 Cor. 12:11).

4. The Spirit reveals right action, wrong action, and calls us to accountability.
    - "[The Spirit], when He comes, will convict the world concerning sin and righteousness and judgment" (John 16:9).
    - "They were unable to cope with the wisdom and the Spirit with which [Stephen] was speaking" (Acts 6:10).

5. The Spirit illumines the Word of God and reveals deep spiritual truth.
    - "The Spirit searches all things, even the depths of God" (1 Cor. 2:10).
    - "We have received ... the Spirit who is from God, so that we may know the things freely given to us by God ... things ... taught by the Spirit" (1 Cor. 2:10).

6. The Spirit works through us despite our limitations.
    - "The Spirit ... helps our weaknesses" (Rom. 8:26a).
    - "My grace is sufficient for you for (My) power is perfected in (your) weakness" (2 Cor. 12:9).

7. The Spirit prays on our behalf.
    - "The Spirit Himself intercedes for us with groan-
      ings too deep for words" (Rom. 8:26b).
    - "Because you are sons, God has sent forth the Spirit
      of His Son into our hearts, crying, 'Abba! Fa-
      ther!'" (Gal. 4:6)

8. The Spirit guarantees our place in God's family.
    - "God ... sealed us and gave us the Spirit in our
      hearts as a pledge" (2 Cor. 1:21-22).
    - "Do not grieve the Holy Spirit of God, by whom
      you were sealed for the day of redemption" (Eph.
      4:30).

9. The Spirit resists the inappropriate desires and cravings
   of the flesh.
    - "The Spirit (sets its desire) against the flesh"
      (Gal. 5:17).
    - "The weapons of our warfare are not of the flesh,
      but divinely powerful for the destruction of
      fortresses (2 Cor. 10:4)

10. The Spirit transforms us into the image of Christ.
    - "We all ... beholding as in a mirror the glory of the
      Lord, are being transformed into the same image
      from glory to glory, just as from the Lord, the
      Spirit" (2Cor. 3:18).
    - "Are you so foolish? Having begun by the Spirit, are
      you now being perfected by the flesh?" (Gal. 3:3)
    - If you are a Christian, then the Holy Spirit is all
      over your life. Listen to His inner voice. Trust Him
      to work through you as you obey the commands of
      Christ. Depend on His help as you attempt great

things for God. Christians don't go at life on their own. To the contrary, the Spirit lives in us and through us. It's not a feeling — it's a fact. Now, go at life in light of that fact!

For Further Study

Adams, Moody. *Jesus Never Spoke in Tongues.* Baker, LA: Moody Adams Evangelistic Association, 1974.

Baxter, Ronald. *Gifts of the Spirit.* Grand Rapids: Kregel Publications, 1983.

Connell, John S. *Aware at Last: Keys to Spiritual Gifts.* Columbus, Georgia: Brentwood Christian Press, 1994.

Carroll, B. H. *The Holy Spirit.* ed. J. B. Cranfill. Nashville: Broadman Press, 1939.

Carson, D. A. *Showing the Spirit: A Theological Exposition of I Corinthians 12-14.* Grand Rapids: Baker Book House, 1987.

Edgar, Thomas. *Miraculous Gifts: Are They for Today?* Neptune, NJ: Loizeaux Brothers, 1983.

Evans, Tony. *The Promise: Experiencing God's Greatest Gift – the Holy Spirit.* Chicago: Moody Press, 1996.

Gilbert, Larry. *Team Ministry: A Guide to Spiritual Gifts and Lay Involvement.* Lynchburg, VA: Church Growth Institute, 1987.

Graham, Billy. *The Holy Spirit: Activating God's Power for Your Life.* Waco: W Publishing Group, 1988.

Hemphill, Kenneth S. *Spiritual Gifts: Empowering the New Testament Church.* Nashville: Broadman Press, 1988.

Ingram, Chip. *Holy Transformation: What It Takes for God To Make a Difference in You.* Chicago: Moody Publishers, 2003.

Leavell, Landrum, II. *The Doctrine of the Holy Spirit.* Nashville: Convention Press, 1983.

MacArthur, John. *Speaking in Tongues: I Corinthians 13:14:40.* John MacArthur's Bible Studies. Panorama City, California: Word of Grace Communications, 1988.

———. *Spiritual Gifts: I Corinthians 12.* John MacArthur's Bible Studies. Chicago: Moody Press, 1983.

———. *The Convicting Ministry of the Holy Spirit.* John MacArthur's Bible Studies. Panorama City, California: Word of Grace Communications, 1989.

————. *Whatever Happened to the Holy Spirit?* John MacArthur's Bible Studies. Panorama City, California: Word of Grace Communications, 1989.

Martin, Ralph P.. *The Spirit and the Congregation: Studies in I Corinthians 12-15.* Grand Rapids: William B. Eerdmans Publishing Company, 1984.

Murray, Andrew. *God's Power for Today.* New Kingsington, PA: Whitaker House, 1997.

Stanley, Charles. *The Wonderful Spirit-Filled Life.* Atlanta: Thomas Nelson Publishers, 1992

Stott, John R. W. *Baptism and Fulness: The Work of the Holy Spirit Today.* Downers Grove, IL: InterVarsity Press, 1964

Young, J. Terry. *The Spirit Within: Straight Talk about God's Gift to all Believers.* Nashville: Broadman Press, 1977.

Zeller, George. *God's Gift of Tongues: the Nature, Purpose, and Duration of Tongues as Taught in the Bible.* Neptune, NJ: Loizeaux Brothers, 1978.

$\mathcal{I}$ndex

G

Galatians
    3:2-3, 31–32, 213
    4:6, 213
    5:16, 75
    5:17, 57, 60–61, 62, 64, 65, 213
    5:19-21, 71, 72, 73–74, 80
    5:22-23, 74–75, 80
    5:24, 76
Generosity, 74
Genesis
    3:6, 61
    28:16-17, 33
    39:2, 42
    39:21, 42
    41:38, 42
Gentiles, speaking in tongues by, 181–190
Gentleness, 74
Gideon, 43
Gift(s), 41–51
    biblical examples of, 42–43
    confidence increased by, 50–51
    definition of, 45–46
    exercises for refining, 52–53
    joy increased by, 50–51
    ministry as use of, 48–49
    of speaking in tongues, 199–200
    varieties of, 45–50
Giving, gift of, 47
Glorification, 149
God, Holy Spirit as, 44
Goliath, 43
Goodness, 74
Graham, Billy, 49
Gruen, Ernest J., 195–196
Guards, 78–79, 80

H

Habits, 78
Havner, Vance, 64

Health, physical and spiritual, 85–87
Heart
   impressions of
      distinguishing physical *vs.* spiritual, 153–164
      leadership of Holy Spirit through, 147–151
   and mind, in understanding Bible, 14
   opening to God, 148–150
Helping, gift of, 46–47
Henry, Jim, 49
Historical background, for Bible, 133–134
Hollywood, 109–110
Holy Spirit Readiness Quotient (HSRQ), 8–10

I

Idolatry, 73
Ignorance
   of Holy Spirit, 1–2, 32–33
   among non-Christians, 109–110
Incarnation, importance of, 57
Intellectual integrity, as reason for rejecting Jesus, 20–21
Isaiah 59:2, 149

J

Jacob, 33
James
   1:5-6, 148–149
   4:2, 148
   4:3, 149
Jesus Christ
   commitment *vs.* surrender to, 21
   as connection to supernatural, 18, 21
   Holy Spirit as, 44
   how *vs.* what of ministry of, 44–45
   reasons for rejecting, 18–21
   teachings on Holy Spirit, 2–3
Jews
   Gentiles speaking in tongues and, 183–190
   as unbelievers, 183
Job, 29
Joel, Holy Spirit revealed to, 3, 4

O

Old Testament. *See also specific books*
  Holy Spirit in, 3–4, 98

P

Passover
  death angel in, 15–16
  Pentecost and, 15–17
  pilgrimage for, 16–17
  significance of, 15
Patience
  in life controlled by Holy Spirit, 74
  in opening heart to God, 150
Paul. *See specific books of Bible*
Peace
  of impressions of heart, 148
  in life controlled by Holy Spirit, 74
Peanuts comic strip, 5–6
Pentecost
  Passover and, 15–17
  problems with explications of, 13–14
  significance of, 16, 57–58
Peter, 64, 184–188
1 Peter
  2:9, 5
  4:10-11, 47
Physical *vs.* spiritual desire, distinguishing, 153–163
Prayer, tongues not language of, 173–174
Precepts, 128–130, 139
Presenting self to God, 65–67
Principles, 128–130
  characteristics of, 129–130
  definition of, 128
  exercises on, 139
  ways of discovering, 130–136
Prophesy, 5, 202
Psalm 119:99-100, 127

R

Readiness Quotient, Holy Spirit, 8–10

for flesh, 68, 80
on gifts, 52–53
on impressions of heart, 151
on leadership of Holy Spirit, 114
on principles and precepts, 139
on readiness quotient, 8–10
on reconnection, 37
on role of Holy Spirit, 22
for seeing unseen, 93
on spiritual *vs.* physical desire, 163–164
on tongues, 178, 192, 208
on truth, 125

Z
Zeller, George W., 189

Biographical Sketch

John S. Connell is senior pastor of Calvary in Savannah, located in Savannah, Georgia, having also led two other congregations in Georgia and two in Louisiana. In addition to his degree in Business Administration from the University of North Alabama, he earned the Master of Divinity and Doctor of Theology degrees from the New Orleans Baptist Theological Seminary. Dr. Connell has also served as an Adjunct Professor at the North Georgia Center for Theological Studies.

During his training at New Orleans Seminary, the faculty selected Dr. Connell as the Outstanding Master of Divinity Student. He has also been noted in *The Official Register of Outstanding Americans: Special Edition of Southern Baptist Leaders*, as well as the *Marquis Who's Who in Religion*. Dr. Connell's work has appeared in numerous publications, including *The Theological Educator, Proclaim: The Pastor's Journal for Biblical Preaching*, and *The Christian Index*.